CORNCRIBS

In History, Folklife, & Architecture

Keith E. Roe was born and raised on a family farm near Williams, Iowa. He attended Iowa State University and received a bachelors degree in horticulture in 1960. He has graduate degrees in botany from the University of Wisconsin and librarianship from the University of Oregon. Dr. Roe is currently head of the Life Sciences Library at Penn State. His longtime interests in photography and agricultural history led to the creation of this book.

© 1988. Iowa State University Press, Ames, Iowa 50010
All rights reserved

Designed by Joanne E. Kinney

Composed and printed in the United States of America

No part of this book may be reproduced in any form or by any electronic or mechanical means, including information storage and retrieval systems, without permission from the publisher, except for brief passages quoted in a review.
First edition, 1988

Library of Congress Cataloging-in-Publication Data

Roe, Keith E.
    Corncribs in history, folklife & architecture / Keith E. Roe.—1st ed.
    p.   cm.
    Bibliography: p.
    ISBN 0-8138-0364-0
    1. Corn—United States—Storage—Cribs—History.
I. Title. II. Title: Corncribs in history, folklife, and architecture.
TH4935.R64 1988
633.1′568′0973—dc19

For Dad and Mom
(Jim and Martha)

Contents

PREFACE / ix

ACKNOWLEDGMENTS / xi

1
INTRODUCTION / 3

2
COLONIAL PERIOD / 11

3
PIONEER SPIRIT AND WESTWARD EXPANSION / 21

4
TWENTIETH CENTURY: ERA OF GROWTH / 36

BIBLIOGRAPHY / 96

PHOTOGRAPHIC CREDITS / 100

INDEX / 101

Preface

This book illustrates the history of corn storage from the earliest records to the mid–twentieth century. For the most part it is the story of the corncrib as a feature of the American farmstead. Because the structures themselves tell their story best, this is first and foremost a picture book. I have also drawn upon the works of many authors, in addition to my own recollections of farm life and carpentry, to add perspective to the illustrations. There exist many unusual or unique corncribs and I have included some of these; but for the most part I have intentionally emphasized the more common types.

The recorded history of corn storage structures, like that of many everyday objects, is scattered and often accidental. People living their daily lives hadn't the time and rarely felt the need to record ordinary details of their utilitarian buildings or routine farming operations such as corn harvesting and storage. Farmers and carpenters were generally too busy to write much. We often have to content ourselves with fragments of what it was like in bygone times, gleaned from diaries, notes, artifacts, and recollections of individuals who lived then. Historians, too, have in the past tended to ignore the ordinary. History, it would seem, is made by warriors and governments if one is to judge from textbooks. Yet cultures are made up of ordinary people. Recently, cultural geographers, folklife specialists, and historians have been attracted to social history, that of common people and their ways and means of life.

The idea for this book came in 1980 while traveling near my boyhood home in central Iowa. It occurred to my wife that I ought to put my interests in photography and agricultural history together with remembrances of helping my dad build corncribs in the late 1950s, working summers between school years with his carpenter crew. It seemed worthwhile to record in pictures what appeared to be a vanishing landmark of midwestern farmsteads. This grew into a broader interest in corn storage from its earliest times and a fascination for the diversity and regional differences among existing corncribs. By coincidence my dad was also an amateur photographer back in the teens and twenties. Several of his pictures taken on glass plate negatives with a Conley view camera are included here. The resulting work aims to give the general reader a concise historical account of the storage of corn, America's most important crop. The book is not intended as a definitive history but perhaps may provide a glimpse of it and stimulate more scholarly works.

Because the most eventful history of ear corn storage occurred in the twentieth century, this part of the story is not only the longest but in a way the hardest to tell. Recent history is tricky to write because there are so many people out there who still remember living it—and each one remembers it a bit differently. Consequently I have written part of the recent history from my own perspective. I do not necessarily mean to tell it as others might remember, nor is it meant to represent a consensus of opinion by established authorities on the subject.

The field work leading to this book heightened my interest and that of my wife in farmstead architecture generally. I hope the book will likewise help readers on future drives through the countryside to observe the rural landscape with a greater perspective for the history that has preceded them.

Acknowledgments

I am indebted to many generous individuals who helped me with this project. Special acknowledgments are due those who went beyond expectations to provide information, advice, or illustrations for this book. I take full responsibility, however, for how I might have used or misused their material or advice. In describing one thread among the weave of life, one can only hope not to have "wronged the write" of history too much. A special thanks is extended to the many, and mostly unknown, farmers who encouraged my efforts and offered their farmsteads as photographic subjects. For their recollections of details about construction I am grateful to Dad and my brothers James and Raymond who were carpenters along with him. I am thankful, too, for parents who were always the greatest of supporters. Lastly I must pay tribute to my wife, Eunice, not only for inspiring the book and for her editorial advice but for helping me spot many special corncribs in our sojourns, and to our children, Eric and Susan, who tolerated vacation travels that somehow became photographic sessions, often it seemed along the hottest stretches of road.

A six-month sabbatical from the Pennsylvania State University enabled me to complete the writing and preparation of the photographs for this book.

CORNCRIBS

In History, Folklife, & Architecture

1
Introduction

Maize, America's corn and major gift to the world's food crops, has sustained people for five thousand years or more. Corn has been cultivated, harvested, and stored in many ways over these centuries. Today's methods of husbandry and facilities for storage bear little resemblance to those of even fifty years ago, let alone the practices of ancient corn farmers. Massive technologies and machinery now harvest the golden grains, transport and store them in quantities of tons or millions of tons. The days of hand planting, husking, and shelling are long past. So, too, is the era of ear corn storage in the traditional corncrib.

Ironically, corn provides its own natural storage facility. It is one of the easiest grains to keep. Corn may be left standing in the field or shucked and left in piles with little or no immediate damage. When air dried, the ears of corn with their protective layers of husk become natural storehouses for the grains. Indeed, the corn ear is so effective at this that it prevents self-seeding, unlike other cereal grains whose ears or heads shatter naturally, dispersing the seeds. Corn no longer exists in the wild. It survives as a cultivar and food crop only by the intervention of farmers who over the centuries have harvested, husked, stored, and planted the grain.

The story of corn storage would be a simple one were it not for the two factors of advancing technological cultures and competition for the grain from vermin, mold, and other pests. With ever larger human populations and necessary food production came the need for greater storage facilities and innovative means of preservation. Corn production, harvest, and storage are intimately tied to the social changes that have occurred since Amerindians in Mexico first discovered the grain. Some of the cultural changes themselves resulted from the availability of this new food. It altered life-styles and nutritional habits and allowed concentrated populations to exist in cities for the first time on the North American continent. Drying the corn crop and keeping it from birds, squirrels, rats, and other pests is a story of innovation, success, and sometimes failure.

Historically, the corncrib has been one of the most common buildings on American farms east of the Great Plains, yet it has received little of the attention given barns in general. Perhaps this is because of its more singular function. Also it hasn't the nostalgia of the barn. Farmstead architecture of all types has been characterized by the practical, of course, and the corncrib is the essence of utility. Yet folk architecture, including corncribs, is not without innovation, even decoration.

American folk craft and architecture are seen in corn storage structures until well into the twentieth century when manufactured wood-framed, steel-covered structures began to spell an end to vernacular form. Until midcentury, however, rural carpenters continued to design and build corncribs and granaries from their own knowledge, following patterns they were familiar with and perhaps adopting useful features they might see in other localities or in farm publications. This was the case until the 1960s, when corn harvest and storage technologies changed dramatically and at the same time rising lumber prices made all-wood farm structures prohibitively expensive to build.

The growth of American agriculture is reflected in its farm buildings. Perhaps no single feature characterizes this growth better than the corncrib, at least in the Midwest. As American as the crop itself, corncribs trace their ancestry to pre-Columbian days. Advanced Indian civilizations such as the Aztecs of Mexico had log and stone granaries. Early European explorers saw Indian corn stored in houses fashioned from saplings bound together with strips of hickory bark and set above the ground on poles to keep them out of reach of squirrels and mice. More common among the Indians of drier climates, however, was underground storage of crops in pits that were both conservative of building materials and more easily concealed from enemies, whether animal or human. Nevertheless, aboveground corn houses of cane or poles were in use among indigenous Americans from Canada to Florida long before these geographic names were applied to the region.

European settlers arriving in America quickly adopted the native Indian corn as a staple food crop for humans and feed for livestock. Substituting corn for their familiar wheat, the colonists' eating habits changed overnight to avert starvation. Trade with the Indians for their corn was crucial to survival in the initial years of settlement. The colonists first stored their corn in baskets in their hovels, later in lofts over their kitchens. Within a decade they had built crude barns to house their cattle and in the South to dry tobacco. Their corn for feed was kept there in piles or in bins. Only later did separate corn houses or cratches exist and not until the year 1681 does the term "corn cribb" itself appear to be in general use.

Corncribs were apparently common in the colonies by the last two decades of the seventeenth century. The Indian method of storing corn in underground pits or mounds, though well known among the colonists, was not adopted by them for grain storage but did become the food cellar.

In the westward migration of settlers the corncrib developed along with other farm buildings according to the needs and folk architecture of each region. Eighteenth- and nineteenth-century corncribs of the northern states were commonly the keystone or v-shaped structures often regarded as "pioneer" in style yet still very much in evidence today in some regions. Southern cribs of this time were typically made of logs.

The corncrib changed little in appearance during most of its first three hundred years of existence, mainly because harvesting methods remained dependent upon hand labor. In the second half of the nineteenth century, however, stirrings of agricultural growth were occurring in response to an increasing population, settlement of new lands under homesteading, and bringing markets closer to producers via railroads. Mechanization was also seeking its growing role in corn production and harvest by the late 1800s.

Corncribs might be said to have characterized the agricultural growth of the Midwest if not the entire eastern half of the United States throughout its history. However, it is the rapid advances of twentieth-century agriculture that are best symbolized by parallel growth of the corncrib, culminating in the exponential growth decades between 1930 and 1960. Mechanization, hybrid corn, and commercial fertilizers, taken together, pushed the corncrib to the limits of its size, engineering strength, and economy.

The corncrib witnessed the trend to massive cash-crop and export agriculture in the 1960s and 1970s, but it did so from the sidelines for it had by then become obsolete almost overnight by picker/shellers and more decisively by the combine with corn head. Steel grain bins and concrete storage elevators for shelled corn largely replaced ear corn storage in cribs.

The history of the corncrib thus predates modern American history itself, but it ends abruptly after a climactic growth period during the heyday of cheap energy, lumber, and labor. As a farmstead feature of our eastern and midwestern states, the corncrib is both ubiquitous yet rapidly disappearing. This is especially true in the heart of corn country where many of the largest cribs have either been converted to grain storage or now stand empty, replaced by grain-handling systems of bins and auger conveyers. Others are simply burned and bulldozed to make way for new farm buildings or to eliminate them as obstacles and help square up the fields. The corncrib does indeed reflect much of American agricultural growth, displaying the cultural and economic changes that molded a nation from the soil and the golden-eared maize.

The story of corn storage begins before historical records were kept in the New World. We must rely upon archeological evidence and observations of early explorers for this part of the story. In length of time it is the longest and it witnessed remarkable development of diverse corn varieties and practical storage methods by the native American cultures. Unfortunately, only fragments of evidence remain for us to appreciate and to wonder about.

Indian Corn and Storage

The history of Indian corn in North America began with its domestication from wild ancestors over five thousand years ago in central Mexico. Corn's origin has long been a mystery and subject of speculation. Most recently a theory has emerged that is consistent with the archeological evidence for the sudden appearance of corn and its rapid adoption as a food crop. According to botanist Hugh Iltis, corn's ancestor is the grass teosinte that underwent a rapid, catastrophic sex change making the tassel a seed-bearing structure and condensing it into an ear (seed-bearing tassels are not uncommon even among today's hybrids). Such a plant must have caught the attention of early farmers who began cultivating it.

Native Mexicans added maize and beans to their basically meat diet during the Coxcatlan period, about 3500 to 5000 B.C. By 400 A.D. maize or corn, the noble grass, had found its way north and east, passed from one Indian nation to another. The prehistoric Basket Makers of our Southwest were growing much corn by then as their descendants have ever since. Corn reached eastern North America during the Middle Ages as measured by European history. New England tribes had developed their maize agriculture by 1000 A.D. Corn was a major agricultural crop throughout the eastern half or two-thirds of North America some eight-hundred to one-thousand years ago.

All major types of corn had been developed through selection by native Americans long before the European conquest. The oldest type is popcorn, dating from before 3000 B.C. Flint, flour, and the more familiar dent corn came later, but all existed by 1200 A.D. What we call sweet corn because of its concentration of sugar rather than starch is derived from dent corns.

In its course of travel corn was added to the crops already cultivated by the natives, such as pumpkins, sunflowers, and beans. It helped change nomadic hunter-gatherer cultures into more sedentary ones cultivating sizeable fields. Corn supported large human populations and made cities possible, such as those of the Aztecs and Mayas of Mexico, the ancient Navajo and Pueblo nations of our Southwest, and the Mississippi valley Mound Builders. Indian tribes would continue the hunt and they would gather wild fruits, acorns, and nuts, but the revolution in their diet brought about by corn would alter their life-styles and nutrition permanently.

The reliance on corn gave the Indians a diet high in carbohydrates but deficient in protein. Corn protein lacks two essential amino acids, lysine and tryptophan (high protein corns are now being developed by plant breeders). This deficiency was made up for in the Indian diet by adding complementary protein plants such as beans and avocados. The growing dependence on corn may have been deleterious to the health of tribes which did not add such complementary proteins to their diets. Archeologists find increased stress and early death among advanced Indian nations of the Mississippi valley. They point out, however, that the poorer health suffered by these people may not have been due directly to corn itself but to infectious diseases spread by widened trade contacts and to highly organized and crowded living conditions in the cities made possible by maize agriculture.

By the time Europeans arrived in North America the indigenous peoples they encountered were established tillers of the soil as well as hunters. Women had long since assumed the primary role of America's first farmers in many Indian nations; men retained the role of hunter, especially in large-game areas of the North and East.

Indian families and villages produced a lot of corn. Contemporary accounts of the colonists and military records on the destruction of corn in fields and in storage indicate that typical villages had dozens to hundreds or even thousands of acres of corn under cultivation and hundreds or thousands of bushels in reserve. Yields of 20 to 45 bushels per acre were normal. In 1609 Henry Hudson described a great corn harvest drying in piles near Indian houses along the river in New York later to bear his name. He estimated the quantity as enough to load three ships. Champlain in 1610 observed corn drying on the tops of Indian houses and estimated a three- to four-year supply. Even if we discount the probable exaggeration of military reports and boasting of explorers it appears that the Indians were producing vast quantities of corn on their well-tended fields. It has been estimated from observations of the time that a typical New England Indian family might produce and store for its use nearly 1700 pounds of corn annually. Their per capita consumption of the grain is estimated at about 100 pounds more than ours today.

Nations such as the Iroquois grew and stored more corn than they could consume and thus had a surplus for trade with other tribes or to help out families and villages having ill luck with their crops. Community storehouses of corn were also maintained by southeastern Indians for these purposes. William Bartram described such a crib or granary in his travels through the Carolinas from 1773 to 1777. Families made contributions to the "king's crib" as he called it according to ability or inclination.

Productivity under continuous cropping was maintained by using fish as fertilizer in areas where these were abundant. This was more efficient than having to clear new fields every few years by girdling and burning the trees, though the practices of abandoning fields or fallow farming were also common. Along flood plains soil fertility was maintained by the annual deposit of topsoil from the river overflow.

It is significant that all of this corn was destined for use as human food since the Indians had no livestock prior to Spanish introduction of the horse. Their dogs did eat some corn but this was not significant. More was lost to birds, mice, and squirrels. The size of the Indian corn storage, America's first "reserve grain program," can be appreciated by the fact that in the years 1540 to 1542 Hernando de Soto was able to lead his army of 620 men and horses, accompanied by hundreds of swine, through Florida, Georgia, and westward plundering Indian corn supplies for rations. His army would clearly have had difficulty "travelling on its belly" through untilled wild lands.

As corn was brought north and east from its home in Mexico the systems of storing the crop came with it or were adapted from local storage methods for other crops. More than seventeen types of granaries are known from Mexico before the conquest. The Aztec nation had granaries and bins resembling log corncribs. If adequately dried either by air or by heating or parching over a fire, corn would keep in storage on the ear or shelled. The term "shelled," by the way, comes from European explorers who observed Indians using clam shells to remove kernels from the cob.

In the dry Southwest and Mexico, corn was usually dried on the ear first, then sometimes shelled for storage. The husked ears were piled atop houses, sunshades, or "ramadas." These were platforms set on poles to discourage squirrels and mice and to help with ventilation. In other cases the corn was dried on the ground or upon piles of brush. The Pueblo Indians spread their husked corn on roofs, platforms, or on the ground to dry. When air dried, the corn was stacked in storerooms like cordwood, sorted as to color and quality. During the husking process select quality seed ears were set aside with some husks left attached. These were later braided into large traces, each of a single color and often weighing 100 pounds, which then were suspended from beams in the storehouse out of reach of mice.

Indian nations of the dry American Southwest and Mexico also stored their corn in adobe bins or rooms built under protective, overhanging cliffs. Hidden caves and cellarlike rooms, holding jars and baskets of corn, were also used. The Mayan "chultuns" were special underground storage chambers for corn and other foods.

Not all Indians hid their stored corn from enemies. Granaries of the Yuman were large bottomless baskets woven from cordlike twists of willow branches. These measured 3 to 6 feet in diameter, 2 to 5 feet tall, and were placed upon platforms or ramadas. The Pima Indians had granaries resembling bird nests or beehives about 18 inches tall by 3 feet in diameter made from coiled bunches of arrowweed. Another characteristic granary of Mexico is the vase-shaped earthenware urn, often set upon a stone base and having a roof of thatch. The smooth outward tapering sides discourage rodents from finding entrance. Some urns are quite large. The existence of granaries perched in trees has been disputed but certainly trees have been used as temporary storage places, especially for meat from the hunt but also for corn.

1.2 Ramada from Arizona in 1935, used to store corn. Cloth on pole serves as a scarecrow.

1.1 Mexican highland log-type granary for ear corn used by the Aztec Indians during the preconquest period.

1.3 Indian women husking and drying corn in Arizona, 1903.

1.4 Large vase-shaped granary with thatch roof from Morelos, Mexico, 1962.

1.5 Corn drying in trees, Guatemala, 1964.

INTRODUCTION 7

Seed corn received special attention, being stored after shelling in pottery jars called "ollas" or in gourds by Indians of the Southwest. Different colors and varieties of corn were usually planted and stored separately. The Mandans of the Missouri valley kept at least thirteen varieties pure by isolated plantings.

When corn reached the Mississippi and Ohio valleys it was stored in hollow trees and in the concealed, underground pits that had been used by the hunter-gatherer tribes of the region for ages to store acorns and nuts. Similar underground storage pits or bins are known to have been used by early agricultural societies in many parts of the world. Indeed, until the early nineteenth century, pit storage was one of the primary methods of long-term preservation of grain. In the Jordan valley seed-eating peoples of Mallaha made plastered storage pits some twelve thousand years ago. If sealed tightly enough, these pits excluded oxygen and retained the carbon dioxide produced by the respiring grain and any insects present. This prevented destruction by mold or bacteria and likewise killed the insects. In a way these pits are the forerunners of modern airtight sealed bins of the Harvestore type.

The underground storage pit or granary was well known to the Indians. It was called "cuescomates" by the Navajo, a word derived from the Aztec "Cuexcomates." The Mohawk word for making such a store is "asaton," the Seneca called it "wae'sado." French trappers in Canada learned to store their furs in such hidden dugouts or "caches" as they called them. The pit or cache was the most widely used Indian method of corn storage in the North and East. Storage pits were used by Plains Indians along the Missouri, tribes of the Great Lakes region, and those along the East Coast. If properly dried and not contaminated by moisture, corn would keep for two years or more in such pits.

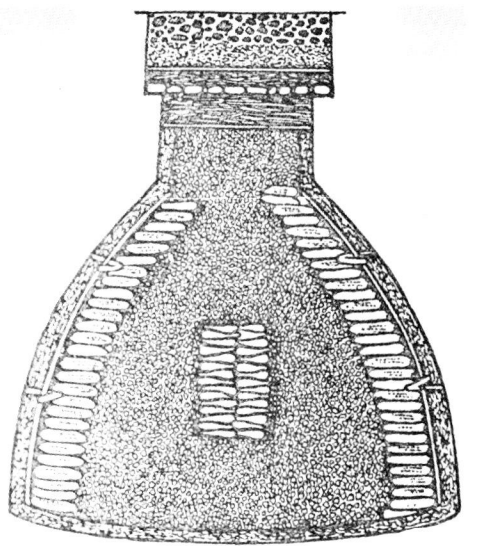

1.6 Cross section of Hidatsa, Plains Indian, cache pit. Used to store corn and dried vegetables.

These dug storehouses were of many types but commonly were jug-shaped, the larger ones 4 to 8 feet deep and of 20 to 30 bushels capacity. They were nearly as broad as deep and had a neck reaching the surface only wide enough for a person to enter. Smaller pits might be only 2 to 3 feet deep and held about 10 bushels. Pits were lined with dry grass, mats, and bark or with clay that might be baked hard to make the structure more waterproof. The pit was filled with mature air-dried corn, both shelled and on the cob, along with beans, nuts, dried meat or fish, berries, and strips of pumpkin. Much corn was picked green, of course. This was either eaten fresh or smoked and dried by hanging it by the husks over fires in the Indian houses. Green corn was also parched until somewhat blackened and then stored in pits. In some cases the shelled corn was first put into skin bags. Pits might also contain whole squashes and pumpkins for winter storage, a system of preservation later copied by white settlers in the form of their food cellars.

Underground pits were especially popular among seasonally nomadic tribes because they could be hidden from enemies when villages were deserted. Once their entrances were covered with earth or sod and made indistinguishable from the surrounding area, these storerooms were secure enough for a tribe to leave its village on a summer hunt or to find milder climates with the approach of winter.

Valuables other than food, such as heavy clay pots or mortars, might also be entrusted to the security of the cache. Wandering bison herds, squirrels, or crows would pass over the caches while marauding Indians would not detect them. At least some would escape notice and be there to sustain the village upon its return. Pit storage was common among the Plains Indians because of a general scarcity of wood for construction.

When pits became infested with mold or no longer kept produce dry they were filled in with trash and new pits dug. These abandoned pits have become today's archeological treasure, yielding information on food habits, pottery styles, and the social structure of the village itself.

1.7 Storage pit near perimeter of house of Mississippi Mound Builders dating from about 900 A.D. Excavation at Dickson Mounds, Illinois. Circular trench held pole frame of house.

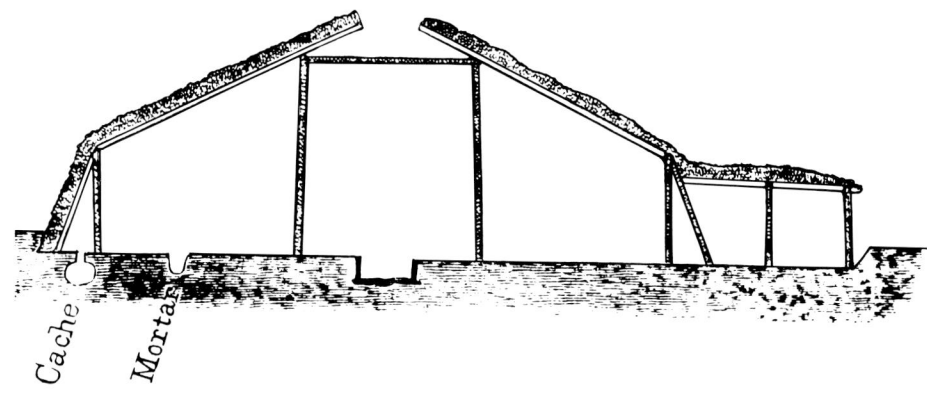

1.8 Cross section of a circular house similar to above showing pit locations — cache for storage, mortar for grinding.

Underground caches were numerous, each family of a village having several. Some might be inside the lodge while others were dug outside but nearby. Occasionally these are uncovered intact even today, still holding the carbonized remains of corn. The pits remain much as their owners left them before succumbing to the epidemic diseases contracted from European fur trappers and colonists.

Practical as underground storage was, larger granaries or storehouses were built aboveground by more densely populated cultures like the Mound Builders of the Mississippi valley. Centered around an extensive city represented today by the Cahokia Mounds east of St. Louis, which date from 1000 A.D., many outlying towns along the Mississippi and Illinois rivers were supported by an extensive floodplain agriculture. Indian tribes of the region had long represented advanced cultures, engaging in distant trade as far as the Rocky Mountains for copper, obsidian, and grizzly teeth and the Gulf coast for hoes of shell and clay pipes. Their storehouses were of pole construction with protective thatch roofs and with bins for ear corn. These were similar in function to the storehouses from Florida illustrated by Jacques Le Moyne in 1564 or 1565.

Traveling along the St. Lawrence River in 1535, the French explorer Cartier observed the Iroquois Indians drying and storing corn atop their houses in "garrets." These garrets would have been similar in function, if not in form, to the ramadas of southwestern Indians. It is worth noting that the term "garret" later came to mean "attic," and here is where the early colonists stored their corn.

Henry Hudson described a corn house of the New Netherlands Indians as "well constructed of oak bark and circular in shape with the appearance of being built with an arched roof. It contained a great quantity of maize from last year."

Hurons and Iroquois of the Great Lakes region stored large quantities of shelled corn in huge bark casks within their longhouses. These casks held 50 to 60 bushels and were infested with innumerable mice and were vulnerable to fires. Consequently, pit storage was used for part of the crop, especially the essential seed corn. One observer, impressed by the colorful nature of Indian corn, noted that prior to shelling, rows of corn ears braided together by their husks into traces hung like tapestry along the length of the Iroquois longhouses.

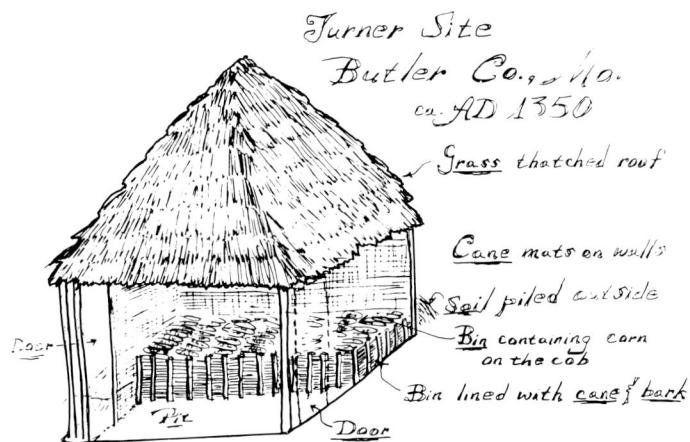

1.9 A corn house or public storage facility of the Mississippi Mound Builders. Structure is square, approximately 2.5 meters on a side. Walls are of pole, covered with cane mats. Roof is thatched grass. Entire structure is built into an excavated basin approximately 35 centimeters in depth.

1.10 Indians of Florida bringing harvest, including corn, to the public granary. This engraving from a drawing in 1564 or 1565 is one of the earliest we have of corn.

1.11 Iroquois longhouse made of bark, corn braids drying on pole. Drawing by a young Seneca, Jesse Cornplanter.

1.12 Bamboo corncrib, Guatemala, 1978.

Other Seneca Indian storehouses were described in 1724 by Father Lafitau as made of bark in tower shape, the bark pierced on all sides to allow air to pass through. Corn houses of the Santee Indians of North Carolina were said by John Lawson in 1701 to be tight-fitting bins set upon eight posts about seven feet high and sealed with clay daubing to keep out insects. Lawson, by the way, was both an observant naturalist and a land dealer. Not surprisingly, perhaps, he was captured by Tuscarora Indians who accused him of stealing their land. They ceremoniously "stuck him full of fine small splinters of torch-wood like hog's bristles and so set them gradually afire."

Corncribs of cane or saplings lashed together and set aboveground upon poles were also used by tribes of the humid Southeast. These were likely similar to the corncribs seen today in less developed regions. In the tropics they may be made almost entirely of bamboo. Such a structure is described by a Portuguese "Gentleman of Elvas," chronicler of de Soto's rampage through the Southeast in 1540 to 1542, as "a maize crib, made of cane, called by the Indians barbacoa." He goes on to say that "Maize is kept in a barbacoa, which is a house with wooden sides, like a room, raised aloft on four posts, and has a floor of cane."

Barbacoa is a prehistoric West Indian Arawak word from which comes our "barbecue." It was used by the Indians to describe a variety of raised platforms. It could designate a bed or a grid upon which meat or corn were dried or roasted by fire from beneath. Southern tribes were also known to make fires beneath their corncribs not only to help dry the ears but to create smoke that discouraged insects. Parching did much the same. Artificial drying was reinvented in the nineteenth century by using a kerosene stove to heat the crib and, as we will see, heat and forced air helped displace the corncrib in the mid–twentieth century.

It seems clear that the Indians built and used corncribs and granaries little different from those of later generations. But whether the European colonists in America adopted crib storage of corn directly from the Indians is more questionable.

2
Colonial Period

Barns and other farm outbuildings were not the first concerns nor even the most critical needs of the early seventeenth-century English settlers who founded the Virginia and Massachusetts colonies. Higher priorities were food and crude shelters, a fortress or stockade for protection, and a common storehouse for the food and supplies brought with them.

The first successful English colony in America was Jamestown in Virginia, settlers arriving there in 1607, some twenty years after the "Lost Colony" failure at Roanoke Island, North Carolina. The Virginia colonists were not farmers. Indeed, they expected to receive provisions from the London Company which had sent them into this wilderness. If agriculture had been a priority, the Jamestown site probably would not have been chosen since it is low lying, swampy, and infertile. When supplies failed to arrive and famine threatened, it was only the corn obtained from friendly Indians by the resourceful but vexing Capt. John Smith that kept the settlers alive the first year.

The first white farmer in Jamestown arrived in 1608, and feeble attempts were made by the colonists that year to grow their own food, especially the wheat, barley, and peas that had been familiar crops in England. These all failed. By 1609 the hungry colonists were willing to plant corn and to learn from two Indians, Kemp and Tassora, how to go about it.

Starvation was still with the colony, however, and during the winter of 1609 all livestock that had been brought over during 1607 to 1608 or subsequently raised was slaughtered for food, including cattle and horses and whatever swine had not escaped to the wilds. Even cannibalism was resorted to by this desperate lot in a land of plenty.

It took strong measures and discipline to turn the miserable situation around and this began in 1611 with the arrival of a new governor and shipments of cattle and hogs. The colonists, who were accustomed to leisure even in the face of starvation, were put to work repairing their dilapidated shacks and fences; making clapboards, pitch, and potash for export to England; and planting corn. Better sites were chosen for the crop, including the cleared fields seized from the Indians. By 1614, 500 acres were planted to corn in community fields. Jamestown in 1615 had three large and substantial storehouses, 120 feet long by 40 feet wide.

Fences or "pales" were always a concern of the colonists and often subjects of dispute as seen in early court records. Not only did fences supposedly define boundaries to be respected by whites and Indians alike, they were meant to enclose and protect the crops. Corn was fenced in while cattle grazed the common meadows and hogs roamed the woods. The swine were especially bothersome in breaking into fields, and pinning the blame on their owners or "keepers of the fence" took much of the court's attention.

Raising crops had not been the original purpose of the Virginia colony. It was intended as a source of raw materials to supply England with needed wood products and precious minerals (unfortunately, the latter did not exist in the area). The colonists expected to become wealthy refining gold and raising silkworms, not merely subsist by farming. Nevertheless, Virginia soon developed an agricultural base. Corn was essential to feed the colonists and their livestock and both it and tobacco became major export crops. Tobacco went to England, corn to the West Indies for the rum and molasses trades.

During the early years of high prices, tobacco growing was so favored by the colonists that restrictions had to be placed on its production. To assure an adequate food supply for the colony a ruling of 1616 stated that each farmer must plant 2 of his allotted 3 acres to corn. In 1619 a law passed by the first assembly to meet in the colony provided that every householder should reserve "in store" a barrel of corn not only for himself but for every servant as well. Still there were shortages of grain, even into the 1630s.

Another commodity the Virginia settlers lacked at first was beer. They had no tavern or beer house and had failed to bring a brewer to the colony. The settlers complained bitterly that they had only water to drink. Ale was their natural drink and indeed a healthier one at that, especially compared with the oft-contaminated water supplies back home. By 1629 two brewhouses had been built and the colonists began to achieve "naturalness" again. Indian corn and barley were malted to make the ale and beer.

Pilgrims on the Mayflower carried provisions of beer but these proved insufficient for the voyage to New England. They landed at Plymouth Rock instead of farther south as was their intent because they had run low on beer; only enough remained for the crew on the return voyage. As one colonist recorded: "we could not now take time for further search or consideration, our victuals being much spent, especially our Beere."

The settlers who arrived at Plymouth, Massachusetts, in 1620 were attracted to New England in part by a glowing account of the region written by John Smith of Virginia fame. However, they differed from the earlier group in their expectations of the country and of themselves. They expected to work in order to eat rather than gain fortune from gold and gems. As in Virginia, however, the New England colonists were not farmers but they were industrious and learned quickly from their Indian hosts.

Arriving late in the year and ill-prepared to face a New England winter, the colonists were fortunate to discover Indian corn stored in pits or mounds. It had been left there by natives whose populations had recently been decimated by European diseases introduced by trappers and explorers. Smallpox was the deadliest but the Indians had no immunity to tuberculosis, influenza, measles, or the rat-carried typhus either. It is estimated that between 75 percent and 90 percent of the Indian population in the region had been lost by 1616 to one plague or another.

The first party to land on Cape Cod in November 1620, under the command of Miles Standish, found Indian fields where maize had recently been harvested. Nearby they saw newly made mounds of earth which they opened and found "a little old basket, full of fair Indian corn; and digged further, and found a fine great new basket, full of very fair corn of this year, with some six and thirty goodly ears of corn, some yellow, and some red, and others mixed with blue, which was a very goodly sight." They took all they could carry away in a kettle found with the corn and filled their pockets as well. The weight of their armor prevented them from carrying more. This cache and others nearby yielded about 10 bushels that the colonists planned to use as seed the following spring.

Farming got underway in 1621 with the advice of the Indian Squanto on how to plant corn and fertilize each hill with fish. Providence seemed to have decreed that the creeks abound in alewives for the netting by cartloads just when needed for springtime manuring of the fields. It took only a few days to catch the fish and plant the corn crop —the difficulty came in keeping the fish in the ground. Edward Winslow complained that Indian corn "will not be procured without good labour and diligence, especially at seed time, when it must also be watched by night to keep the wolves from the fish, till it be rotten, which will be in fourteen days." Village dogs were as much trouble as wolves. In Ipswich it was decreed "that all doggs, for the space of three weeks after the publishinge thereof, shall have one legg tyed up.... If a man refuse to tye up his dogg's legg, and hee bee found scraping up fish in the corne field, the owner shall pay 12s." Twenty acres of corn and 5 acres of peas and barley or wheat were planted that first year on vacant Indian lands. The English grain came to no good but the Indian corn was a success.

No livestock was brought over on the Mayflower in 1620 — it probably wouldn't have survived the winter anyway. Not until 1624 were cattle and goats introduced to the Plymouth Colony. Horses, swine, poultry, and sheep followed in 1627 and by 1630 the settlement of New England was well underway. In 1631 Governor Winthrop of Massachusetts Bay could record "a plentiful crop" of corn. Yet it was still too dear a commodity for general use as feed for livestock. Corn had been valued as barter for years — it was preferred over money in periods of inflation. In 1631 corn was legal tender in Massachusetts, equaling 6s per bushel. A law prohibited feeding this "country pay" to swine except when a plentiful harvest sent the value of the grain below the set rate.

Yields of corn in the decades 1620 to 1640 ran about 18 to 20 bushels per acre though 50 bushels per acre might be produced on fertile ground. The decline in yield on formerly more productive Indian fields was due to poor husbandry, at least until the 1640s when animal manure began to be used as fertilizer by some farmers.

The Dutch colony of New Netherland (New York) was settled beginning in 1625 under the direction of the Dutch West Indies Company. Manhattan, purchased from the Indians in 1626 for 60 guilders, was occupied first while some Dutch farmers moved to Long Island or across the Hudson to begin settlement of New Jersey. Cattle, horses, sheep, and hogs were brought with the settlers. Each colonial family was allotted a "patch" of land and furnished with a house, barn, farming implements and tools, four horses and four cows, and some sheep and pigs. The farmer in return paid a yearly rent of 100 guilders and 80 pounds of butter to the company. At the end of six years he could keep whatever increase he had managed to obtain in the number of his livestock. The Dutch settlers were good farmers and soon were exporting wheat on a commercial basis.

Some early Dutch barns were substantial. One on Long Island, built in 1638, measured 18 by 40 feet and 24 feet high. Yet able carpenters were always in short supply in the early years of the American colonies and architects were unknown before 1685. Advertisements to induce sawyers and carpenters to emigrate were common in the early seventeenth century. Even in 1658 a Dutch settler of New Amsterdam complained: "These would-be carpenters who had come with the first contingent of colonists, were 'bunglers or men of little capacity.'" Most settlers had to do their own carpentry.

The settlement of Maryland commenced in 1634. By this time it was recognized that corn was essential to the survival of a colony and instructions were given for its planting. Livestock were obtained from nearby Virginia and, following the lead of its sister colony, tobacco culture was adopted.

Swedish settlements were established in 1638 along the Delaware river where Wilmington now stands. The Scandinavians were an agricultural people and they adopted corn as a major crop. Out of the white and yellow kinds they made bread while the blue, brown, black, and variegated types were brewed into beer. The Swedes built grain storehouses of round or hewn logs and with roofs of birch bark covered with sod, much like those of their home country. These were raised 2 to 3 feet off the ground for ventilation and to prevent invasion by mice.

The choice of this location for settlement by the Swedes was propitious, it being a gateway to the fertile lands of Delaware, New Jersey, and southeastern Pennsylvania. It was to be the German and Dutch farmers, however, finding refuge in William Penn's colony, who would develop this agricultural area beginning in 1681 and introduce the characteristic large American or Pennsylvania German barn. Writing to the people of England in 1692 about the Province of Pennsylvania, Richard Frame described

> The Fields, most fruitful, yield such Crops of Wheat,
> And other things most excellent to eat.
> As Barley, Rye, and other sorts of Grain,
> In peace we plow, we sow, and reap again,
> Good Indian Corn, which is a larger breed,
> It doth our Cattle, Swine and Horses feed,
> Buck-Wheat and Oats, beside, good store of Reed,
> A plentiful Land, O plentiful indeed, . . .

The Scandinavians left a lasting contribution to farmstead architecture, however. Not only did they introduce the log house to the New World but, as we will see later, their log hayshed and storehouse designs became models for our classic American corncrib.

Two characteristics of American agriculture originated early in the colonies. One is its basically free-enterprise nature, the other a makeup of individual farms. These features were to leave their stamp upon the countryside and help shape American farm buildings for over two centuries.

At their beginnings the American colonies were modeled after the English feudal village, in part out of habit but also due to a perceived and real need for security from unknown natives. In village-style agriculture the houses and outbuildings were clustered together while the surrounding fields were tilled by farmers working out of the community and contributing to it. At least part of the crop was stored in a community storehouse.

Southern farmers soon abandoned this system of group living in favor of individual farmsteads. Large land holdings or plantations did become essentially villages themselves, of course. In New England the village system persisted through the eighteenth century and into the early 1800s, but the great landed estates were largely eliminated as a result of the American Revolution.

Independent-minded settlers of the 1630s and 1640s preferred to disperse inland in order to carry on trade with the Indians rather than tolerate the confines of village life. For many European immigrants the size of their new homesteads in America was larger than the farms they left back in the Old Country, subdivided as they had been

2.1 Log storehouse called a "härbre" from Vamhus, Sweden, dating to 1522 A.D. Such elevated storehouses and granaries are also known from Norway and Finland while very similar structures are found in Bavaria, Austria, and Switzerland. Scandinavians introduced log construction to America beginning in 1638. Raising granaries aloft for ventilation and protection from vermin was a practical discovery among native farmers of both Old and New Worlds.

over the generations. Larger individual farms further encouraged independence and less need to live community style.

Until 1623 the Plymouth Colony had operated under a form of communal governance whereby laborers worked for the community and resources were shared. This was changed during 1623 to 1624 to a free-enterprise system, each family being granted an acreage. Communal government had been tried in the Virginia colony as well. It failed in both areas because of the independent nature of the settlers and the availability of land, free for the taking — from the wilderness or the Indians. Throwing off the shackles of communal and village life, colonial farmers became dis-

2.2 Rural village, "Poestenkill, N.Y., Summer," painted by Joseph Hidley between 1865 and 1872, showing farmsteads clustered together and fields beyond. Note V-shaped corncrib, bottom right.

persed, provincial, and fiercely independent to the point of being self-sufficient.

Except for barns, which did become large in the eighteenth century, farm outbuildings such as those for grain storage remained relatively small, corresponding to production on individual farms and the lack of mechanization. Machinery didn't play a significant role until the rise of large-scale agriculture during the mid to late 1800s. And the central storehouse of early colonial days didn't reappear, albeit in rather different form, until the era of farmer cooperatives with their large grain elevators. Cooperatives are usually considered a twentieth-century development but they do have earlier roots, such as the Granger movement in the late 1800s. Even in 1685 Thomas Budd was advocating public granaries for protection from rats and mice and for cooperative selling.

The first colonial houses were tents, wigwams, huts, or brush and wattle shedlike hovels with roofs of thatch, bark, or mats, patterned after the Indian dwellings. These were replaced as soon as possible by framed timber buildings with clapboard siding and shake roofs. The original hovels might then be used as storage sheds or livestock shelters. Sometimes, however, the temporary housing had to last for several years. Most early colonial houses were small, cheap to build, and poorly constructed—the original American "throwaway." One contemporary observer noted that the houses "fell down again before they were finished."

A basement type of farmhouse was introduced by the Dutch in 1650 as a practical structure for cold New England regions. Settlers would

> dig a square pit in the ground, cellar fashion, six or seven feet deep, as long and as broad as they think proper, case the earth inside all round the wall with timber, which they line with the bark of trees or something else to prevent the caving in of the earth; floor this cellar with plank and wainscot it overhead for a ceiling, raise a roof of spars clear up and cover the spars with bark or green sods, so that they can live dry and warm in these houses with their entire families for two, three and four years.

Later immigrants arriving in Philadelphia from 1682 to 1687 often lived a year or more in caves or holes dug into the banks of the Schuylkill and Delaware rivers. Some thrifty souls took up temporary residence in hollow trees or even large barrels and, as one commentator noted, they have "but one window, and that's the Bung-hole, requiring a Cooper instead of a Carpenter to keep their Houses in repair."

Living in a cellar or basement is not unknown to recent memory. Some families from the 1920s to the 1950s ran into economic problems while building new houses. With only the basement completed they would roof this over, use a cover of black tar paper, and live below ground level, often for years before completing the house. Some were never completed.

The first successful corn crops produced in the American colonies or obtained from the Indians were stored in baskets within the settler's hut or in bins and barrels in the community storehouse. By 1624, when frame houses existed in Virginia, a loft or garret above the kitchen served as a dry place to store corn. Within twenty years after colonization, farmers of Virginia and New England were producing enough corn to warrant storage in lofts or corn bins of the shed or barn. From Delaware south the tobacco house served also to store corn.

Partly for security of the precious grain, colonial farmers did not immediately adopt the Indian method of storing corn in separate cribs. It was easier to guard their grain if kept in the house or barn. And until corn production was sufficient to permit its use as livestock feed, probably in the mid-1630s, the efficient place for storage was near the kitchen. Even in the latter 1600s corn was kept in the "garretts." In 1673 during an attack by the English on the Dutch town of Hoerenkil (now Lewes), Delaware, John Roads's house was set afire. He beat down the gable end to throw out his corn. A letter of 1686 reads "Our Barn, Porch and Shed, are full of Corn this year." The "shed" might have been what we would call a corncrib.

The New England colonists experienced winters far more severe than those familiar to them back home. They were ill-prepared with their own housing, let alone anything for their domestic animals that were left to forage in the woods. Shelter for cattle and pigs had been unnecessary in England. In America, however, the resulting loss of livestock was so great that before many winters passed the settlers were forced to construct simple barns for their domestic animals and for hay and grain storage as production increased.

It is generally acknowledged that the barn was not a significant feature of New England farmsteads until the eighteenth century. Livestock in the southern colonies had to fend for itself even longer. In the German settlements of Pennsylvania, on the other hand, livestock shelter was viewed as a necessity, in part because of tradition in the Old Country. Even here, however, the earliest barns were mere "coverts" or "outhouses" for cattle.

The availability of draft animals, horses and oxen, increased greatly the potential and the need for corn production. Whereas before "it was with sore labour that on(e) man could Plant and tend foure Acres of Indians Graine and now [1637] with two Oxen hee can Plant and tend 30."

From seventeenth-century records it is evident that a house and barn were the only essential buildings of a farmstead. In the North these were of wood frame and rough board siding while from Delaware south unchinked log shelters served as first barns. The term "barne" frequently meant general storage shed as well. Colonial farmers lived with a hodgepodge arrangement of their tools, goods, and produce. The only thing neat about their farmsteads were the "neat" cattle, a term for any common breed of bovine stock. And a "neat" house in those days meant habitable, not necessarily orderly.

Even the Indian storage pits were called "barnes" in New England. In 1674 John Reynolds sued the Pequot sachems or chiefs Wequashcuck and Mamaho for £7 damages, alleging that a cow of his had fallen into one of their barns. The court dismissed his claim.

Along with hay, the barn loft was used to spread corn to dry. Bins were constructed for its storage. Separate corn ricks, bins, corn houses or sheds came later but at least by the mid-1600s as good weather, safety from the Indians, and luck with the corn crop justified them. These were boxlike structures built of logs or saplings notched at their ends or, more simply, of fence rails laid crisscross to form a loose-fitted, ventilated bin. Such cribs have been common even in the twentieth century. The corn house was made of crude frame construction covered loosely with rough-sawn board siding, which allowed for air passage and drying of the corn.

Origin of the term "corncrib" is probably lost to history. Its first known written use is in the Brookhaven (Long Island, New York) town records of 6 June 1681, in a public confession:

"I Hannah Huls, through inadvertance and passion, defamed Nathanell Norten, of this towne, by saying he had stollen Indian corn out of my fatther daiton's his corn cribb."

He was probably referring to Samuel Dayton's corncrib and "fatther" in those days might indicate "employer" or "elder."

An estate inventory of 1682 notes "Indian corn in a crib unthrasht" with a value of £16, easily the most valuable item listed, even surpassing the four oxen at £11.

2.3 Reconstructed from hewn poplar and red oak logs dating to the mid-nineteenth century, this 250 bushel corncrib on the Lincoln Living Historical Farmstead of 1824 is very much like those of nearly two hundred years earlier—a simple bin with board or thatch cover.

Presumably the term "corncrib" was a common expression at least by 1681. Much more familiar, however, from colonial times through the mid–nineteenth century were the terms "corn house" or "corn barne." It was said that corn was "housed," not "cribbed." The term "cratch" also was used until the early 1800s to describe a small corn storage bin or building.

Cratch and crib are both related historically to the old German word "Krippa" or manger. And, of course, both were used in Europe long before the discovery of America. Cratch is an obsolete expression insofar as corn storage goes but may better describe the early ventilated corn storage structures made of fence rails or small logs by our pioneer farmers.

The first simple, boxlike corncribs might have been called "corn bins" or "corn ricks" rather than proper corn "houses," but these terms are not used in seventeenth-century diaries, wills, or official records to describe farmsteads. Actually most official records such as probates of estates mention nothing more than houses, barns, and "sheds," plus "outbuildings" or "outhowses." Presumably what we now refer to as corncribs would have been included here along with haysheds and toolsheds.

The classic American V-shaped corncrib has sides that flare outward toward the top giving the appearance of a keystone or coffin from an end view. The entire structure is generally set above ground on four or more posts. This style of corncrib is seen today especially from New Jersey and Pennsylvania to Ohio and in Wisconsin and Minnesota, areas with historical roots in the Delaware valley or ethnic ties to northern Europe. This style American corncrib originated as a modified European log hayshed of early immigrants.

2.5 Virginia farmer of 1650 shown in this mural by Sidney King at the Jamestown Historical Site, Virginia. Corn shed at left has bins along the wall for ear corn. Farmer is bringing in husked corn for storage from his field in the distance.

2.4 Fence-rail crib with cornstalk cover, Paulding, Ohio, 1916. Except for its large size this same design would have fit in with a farmstead of 1635.

Some northern European haysheds dating from the sixteenth and seventeenth centuries or later have a distinctive V-shape. Their sides flare outward toward the eaves to aid in shedding rain or snow and to keep the hay from packing down. In many the gable ends also flare outward. Contemporary granaries of the region are usually set 2 to 3 feet above the ground on posts or smooth rocks to help keep out rats and to aid in drying.

Immigrants from Sweden and Finland were first to introduce European-style log storehouses, granaries, and haysheds to America beginning in 1638. In his travels through the English colonies in America between 1748 and 1751, the Swedish naturalist Peter Kalm described the maize houses as "similar to our hay sheds…." The distinctive V-shape of our American corncrib owes its origin to these haysheds of Europe. And in placing their corncribs aboveground on four or more posts, immigrant farmers were merely following habits of constructing granaries.

COLONIAL PERIOD 17

2.6 A corn cratch or "rustic corncrib" as it is called in an article by a writer from New Jersey who had little good to say about the average corncrib. His design was for the "country place, not an ordinary farm where the necessary ugliness of the usual corncrib may be substituted by a very pretty and picturesque effect...can be a prominent object in the yard instead of hiding it away, as is often done, behind an outhouse or shed."

2.7 The classic American corncrib. Keystone or V-shaped, usually small, set upon posts. Chisago County, Minnesota 1983.

2.8 Hayshed from Gulf of Bothnia, Finland, 1912. Note that both the sides and gable ends flare outward.

The Indians had corn houses in addition to underground barns or pits, and some of these were raised aboveground on poles. None, however, was apparently shaped like the classic "top-heavy" corncrib, designed — it has been said — to tip over in the wind (strangely, however, few of this type crib are seen to have done so). It has often been assumed that the colonists learned to store corn in cribs from the Indians, yet there is no direct evidence for this. On the contrary, by the time the colonists produced enough corn to store in separate cribs for livestock feed, they simply built crude rail bins or reinvented the Indian corn house after the pattern of granaries and haysheds familiar to them from the Old Country to produce our classic American corncrib.

Part of the mystery regarding colonial farm buildings is that little was written about them in contemporary records and none were drawn. The colonists and their leaders were preoccupied with survival, struggles with the natives, and maintaining order within the community (or even keeping a community of independent-minded settlers together). Concern was with the extraordinary in this wild new world, not everyday life or common buildings. Colonial art hardly exists to show us anything of typical living conditions. Except for sketches of fortresses, practically nothing of the ordinary landscape was drawn in Colonial America. Not until the American primitive or folk period of art in the nineteenth century do we see illustrations of corncribs, such as in the works of Francis Alexander, Joseph Hidley, and Edward Hicks. These are highly stylized, of course, as the names of the period suggest, but they seem to depict the corncrib of the day fairly true to life. A nice record of farmstead architecture is seen in the watercolors of Paul Seifert, a nineteenth-century Wisconsin folk artist who painted farmsteads for hire much like aerial photographers would contract to do in the twentieth century.

Surprisingly, perhaps, a few farm buildings dating from the late 1700s and early 1800s have persisted into the twentieth century, long enough to have been recorded on film by the Historic American Building Survey (HABS) or moved to living history farms. These were built after the close of the colonial period, of course, and likely do not represent average farm structures of the day. They probably survived because they were "special" or particularly well built, not the case with the average shed. However, these buildings do give us some idea of styles existing in the former colonies of the Atlantic Seaboard.

2.10 *The Cornell Farm* (1848) by Edward Hicks, better known for his *Peaceable Kingdom*. Small structure on left side of barn toward front and one on gable end may be corncribs. The three covered structures on right are not wire cribs (which didn't exist then) but hay barracks with movable covers raised upon four poles.

2.9 Reconstructed Finnish hayshed at Old World Wisconsin, 1985. Round logs shown here but hewn logs are also common. Similar haysheds are known from Norway and Sweden.

2.11 A Pennsylvania barn with attached crib similar to the Hicks painting, from Centre County, 1983.

COLONIAL PERIOD 19

2.12 *The Siefert Farm*, Gotham, Wisconsin, by Paul Siefert, about 1880.

2.14 Corncrib (with vertical slats) at Old House of the Hinges, so named because of the large unique hinges on the smokehouse, late eighteenth century, Dorchester County, Maryland.

2.13 Wye House corncrib, Talbot County, Maryland, late eighteenth century.

20 COLONIAL PERIOD

2.15 Corncrib from North Scituate, Rhode Island, now at Old Sturbridge Village, Massachusetts, dating from the late eighteenth or early nineteenth century. Note placement on "staddle stones" for rat protection. Except for vertical siding, the construction here is very similar to that suggested in the King mural at Jamestown, even the corn bin.

2.16 DeClerique Farm Group, Closter, Bergen County, New Jersey, early nineteenth century. Note metal flashing around posts for deterring rats — but ladders for their convenience. Also pigeon holes or dovecotes.

2.17 Corncrib on the Cliffs, Calvert County, Maryland, early nineteenth century. Note cribbing on inside of log timbers. Such heavy framework required little or no inside bracing which made it easy to apply cribbing where it belongs for structural strength. Modern light framework (balloon framing) requires considerable bracing inside; hence the cribbing must be to the outside.

3

Pioneer Spirit and Westward Expansion

The Revolutionary War brought colonialism to an end just as westward expansion was getting fully underway. In 1790, 94 percent of the U.S. population lived in the original thirteen former colonies, newly become states, all east of the Alleghenies. The West included Kentucky, Tennessee, and Ohio. Pushing westward even before British rule ended, the frontier farmer continued practices set down by his colonial predecessors. A few acres were cleared by girdling the trees and corn was planted among the dead snags. The family depended upon game and other wild foods to supplement what they could raise. Indian raids on outlying farmsteads were always a possibility along the frontier and a deterrent to settlement by less adventurous souls.

The new nationalism brought changes to agriculture as well as to government. Farming was becoming more commercialized as potential urban markets grew and as production increased beyond the needs of subsistence or local trade. New scientific and systematic methods of farming, some borrowed from the agricultural revolution taking place in England, were being promoted by recently formed agricultural societies and the new agricultural press. Frequently, however, these societies and publications were more literary than practical; later in the nineteenth century they became more political.

The year 1820 is often cited as pivotal in the transition from self-sufficiency to a market-oriented agriculture in the United States. Agriculture in the eastern states had up to this time been practiced in nearly the same inefficient ways of poor management, especially lack of manuring or crop rotations, common since early colonial days. The East couldn't compete with the attraction of new, cheap lands along the frontier, but being closer to urban markets the opportunity for more efficient farming was there. Progressive farming in the East by midcentury meant efficient management and intensive agricultural practices such as crop rotations with pasture and forage legumes, recovery and use of stable manure, use of mineral fertilizers, and land drainage where necessary, mostly by open ditches.

Perhaps the greatest stimulus to pioneer expansion westward was the series of new federal land policies concerning disposition of the public domain between the Appalachians and the Mississippi River. Controversial from the first in 1785, these laws gradually were molded to fit the interests (or available cash) of would-be small landholders who could afford 80 acres at $1.25 each but not 640 acres. Squatters rights, too, prevailed on public lands until final concession in the Homestead Act of 1862.

The effect of these liberal land policies can be seen by 1850. In the span of sixty years there had been more than a doubling in the number of states, the population had grown sixfold, and the frontier pushed beyond the Mississippi into Iowa and Minnesota and south to Texas. The population was swollen by European immigrants seeking new lands and lives in America, and as this tide pushed westward the frontier was swept ahead of it by Indian land cessions and a vast territorial acquisition, the Louisiana Purchase, in 1803. Settlement of the Midwest really mushroomed after 1840. During the rest of the century the population of thirteen midwestern states increased by five times, corn production by ten times.

Frontier life of the pioneer immigrant was often tough as reflected in stories passed down to second and third generation Americans. There was little cushion between them and the elements, hardly comparable to rural living in the mid-twentieth century. Prairie fires, drought, hail, and grasshoppers worked against the settlers of the Upper Midwest in the 1870s and tested their stamina. Low prices and depressions added to their woes. It hardly does our pioneer farmers justice to say they lived through difficult times. The good old days were yet to come.

Westward-moving farmers of Indiana, Illinois, and Iowa were reluctant to settle on the barren prairies in the erroneous belief that land unable to support trees was not rich enough to produce farm crops. The lack of wood for buildings, fences and fuel, and the scarcity of water were also major deterrents. Too much water was the problem with low-lying wet prairies in these states. The swampy lands were regarded as carriers of ill health for pioneers who settled there. Dysentery, malaria, and typhoid were common ailments caused indirectly by poor drainage. Drainage by tile was expensive and open ditches served the needs of many farmers in these days before large-scale mechanization. Surface drainage did, however, merely divert water to one's neighbor, leading to disputes and bad feelings.

Land drainage on a large scale got underway with the creation of drainage districts in Illinois in the 1860s and 1870s. Iowa followed about ten years later but peak drainage efforts took place after 1900. Nearly half the cultivated land of Illinois is tillable today due to drainage. The tough prairie sod was an added deterrent making the "tall grass" country of Illinois and Iowa unattractive to settlers. It was difficult and expensive to turn into farmland. This led to invention of the sod-busting breaking plow made of steel in the 1850s and 1860s while fence needs were answered with barbed wire, perfected by the 1870s.

Mechanization began stirrings of growth by the mid–nineteenth century and the Patent Office saw a rising tide of inventions after 1850. Still, most farm operations were done by hand or with simple implements. The value of farm implements and machinery on an average Illinois farm in 1850 was $84, in 1860 only $120. Minnesota farmers of 1870 had less than $100 worth of machinery. On the other hand a good team of horses at this time might cost $150 to $300. It cost about $1000 to start a 160 acre prairie farm in the 1850s. Change in mechanization was slow — the average farm in 1900 had only $131 worth of equipment.

Unlike the early colonists who had to be nearly self-sufficient, the pioneer agriculturist of the Midwest in the mid–nineteenth century was growing commercial cash crops from the outset. Income and credit were the ways of economic life or, all too often, of privation due to low commodity prices, drought, and crop pests. The pioneer's available cash was small, barter and credit more common. Most settlers had barely enough cash for harness and wagon, let alone factory-made machinery. Many farmers hired machine work done, borrowed implements, or traded work with neighbors.

Corn production moved gradually into the new lands opened to the Northwest but still at midcentury there was no clearly defined Corn Belt. In 1840 the leading corn states were Kentucky, Tennessee, Virginia, North Carolina, and Ohio. Corn was marketed at this time before rail transport largely in the form of whiskey and hogs. Corn whiskey was economical to ship because of its value in proportion to bulk. Gourdseed, a late-maturing white corn grown in the South, excelled in sweetness and produced 2 quarts more whiskey per bushel than the earlier northern flint corns (Corn Belt dents arose from crosses of these two types, by the way). Hogs could walk to market. Professional drovers brought herds of 5000 hogs to eastern city markets until the meat packing industry developed along the Ohio, giving Cincinnati its nickname "Porkopolis" by 1832. Even in 1850 there were nearly 2000 professional drovers. Corn-fed cattle were also part of a growing agricultural industry in southern Ohio and northern Kentucky by 1840.

The effects of the nineteenth century agricultural revolution were slow in affecting ordinary farmstead architecture, including corncribs. Farm buildings might grow in size and numbers but their styles remained few until late in the 1800s.

The American pioneer farmstead of our eastern forested regions is typified by a log cabin or house, a log barn and a simple, binlike corncrib. The log corncrib is especially characteristic of Appalachia from West Virginia to Georgia where it became the basis for a variety of nineteenth-century log crib-barn designs still evident in the southern mountains. Log barns and corncribs are closely related, the single–pen log barn being equivalent to a corncrib and often used as such. The log crib is versatile. If chinked and a larger door cut, it can become a house. Double-pen and larger barns often have one pen or a bin devoted to ear corn storage.

Corn followed the pioneer westward beyond the Appalachians and crib designs went with it. Along the frontier the first farm buildings were often primitive, hewn out of the forest cleared for fields. The first house might be a wigwam, like those used by settlers at Plymouth or Jamestown. Sometimes the hollow trunk of a huge old tree served as first residence. Hollow sections of trees also became storage barrels and hollow stumps might be boarded over to form primitive corncribs. Another kind of temporary housing was the crude log "shanty" or pole and thatch hovel that sheltered the family until a log house could be built. In many cases this would, in turn, be added to or replaced some years later by a "proper" frame or brick house. The original shanty would have become a piggery by then while the log house might be converted to a stable or cow house.

On the other hand, the log structures of many pioneers were well built, especially the houses of people with a heritage of such construction. The log houses of these settlers were meant to be permanent, though they might be "improved" by clapboard siding at some later date. Their other log structures such as simple animal shelters and corncribs might be less carefully built than their houses, but even some of these have stood the test of time.

True barns and cattle sheds were reportedly uncommon on frontier farms of the Upper Midwest in the 1840s. A temporary barn of midcentury from Wisconsin was described as "about the same type as the haystack we had lived in till we moved into the log house."

The first corncrib on many a pioneer farm of the 1860s was built of saplings or split rails just like those of the colonists over two hundred years earlier. In a letter to the home country written in 1868, one Norwegian immigrant from Iowa described a crib as a square container of fence rails with straw placed in the bottom before filling. Other cribs were simple gable-roofed structures made from saplings or logs.

The keystone-style corncrib was brought to the Upper Midwest around midcentury by Scandinavian immigrants. Some of these cribs were of round or hewn log construction, others of frame and boards. The Swedish writer Gustaf Unonius described a pioneer corncrib in Wisconsin at mid-century as "in appearance usually like the basket of a coal cart." A good description of the keystone design is seen much earlier in *The Complete Farmer*, published in 1793 in London for the British reader:

> To preserve this corn, they make in North America a sort of bins, or cages, which they call corn-cribs, fifteen or sixteen feet long, and five or six wide, widening upwards to the top a foot or more. They are made of sapling poles, three or four inches diameter, framed roughly together by notching the ends where they cross the corners, at such a distance from each other, as but just to keep the ears from falling through, that there may be a free passage of air. These bins stand abroad, and have a slight movable covering, or thatch to keep out the rain.

In addition to corner notching, crib rails were sometimes held together by binding them with hickory bark strips or willow withes. After 1860 when cheap manufactured nails became available and local sawmills more abundant, frame construction was more feasible.

There is no shortage of illustrations from the mid–nineteenth century and later depicting corncribs. For example, artists working for Currier and Ives included them in their many rural scenes. The highly illustrated weeklies such as *Harpers Magazine* showed cribs in some of their numerous woodcuts, so popular before photography's dominance later in the century. The *American Agriculturist* published drawings of corncrib designs and recommendations for their improvement. Farmstead improvements in general were a major objective of nineteenth-century agricultural reformers who sought to make farming more scientific and businesslike.

Barns grew to their characteristic large size in the late eighteenth and nineteenth centuries. In addition to housing livestock and sheltering hay, their lofts became important for drying corn while bins were constructed for its storage. Unlike today's mechanized agriculture, harvesting by hand and corn knife was slow and gradual. Corn was left to dry in the field, then cut and brought to the barn, stalks and all. It was piled in the loft or driveway where the ears would dry further before husking. The ears were then stored for the winter in a bin within the barn or in a separate crib. The husks and stalks became fodder for winter feeding of the cattle. The husking bee or "frolic" was a popular neighborhood event in the nineteenth century as romanticized by contemporary poets and artists. Appearance of the corn husker-shredder in 1885 might have spelled the end for this pioneer social activity but it didn't — cooperative corn shucking continued until well into the twentieth century.

3.2 Two-story corncrib with overhanging roof characteristic of southern smokehouses but not uncommon on log corncribs. The projecting roof did offer some protection from rain or shade from sun while unloading wagons. Rockcastle County, Kentucky.

3.1 Double corncrib of hewn and dovetailed logs, late nineteenth century, Gatlinburg, Tennessee.

3.3 Except for its size the pole and sapling crib in foreground is hardly different from colonial cribs of fence rail. Shown here is a left-pitching scooper. Height of crib is about maximum for scooping from a wagon. Tazewell County, Illinois, 1943.

3.4 Unusual tamarack pole and sapling corncrib from Stearns County, Minnesota, built in 1870.

3.5 Hewn-log corncrib from Stearns County, Minnesota, still used for ear corn. Likely dating to 1870s, constructed of poplar logs and clapboards. Square nails used throughout.

3.6 Keystone-shaped corncrib of round logs, saddle-notch construction, from Sherburne County, Minnesota, dating to about 1890.

3.7 Hewn and dovetailed log construction of keystone design. The Dahlen corncrib from Norwegian homesite, originally built about the 1870s.

3.9 Another idealized sketch of a farmyard showing a veritable parade of livestock. Note ladder propped against crib allowing easy access for rats.

3.8 *American Farm Scenes No. 2*, one of the Currier and Ives series. Lithograph by N. Currier, 1853, F. F. Palmer, artist.

Seventeenth century corncribs had been made of fence rails, unchinked logs (sometimes skinned to lessen the danger of infestation by worms and insects), or of crude framing covered with clapboards or whip-sawn rough siding. Invention of the circular saw in 1820 and its growing adaptability to steam power by midcentury made lumber cheap enough for general use on outbuildings such as corncribs. Still the term "cribbing" for such lumber was not used until 1841.

3.11 Husker-shredders like the Janney were popular well into the twentieth century as they eliminated the hand labor of husking out the corn from shocks.

3.10 *Corn Husking* by Eastman Johnson, 1860. Popularized as a lithograph by Currier and Ives.

3.12 Neighborhood corn shucking and ready to crib, Granville County, North Carolina, 1939.

In constructing a framed corncrib, two ways of attaching the slat siding or cribbing were used. The slats were put on either horizontally or vertically (cribbing attached diagonally for extra strength seems to have come into use about 1900). Vertical application promoted water runoff except for the bottom ends that sometimes rotted out from the moisture collecting there. Horizontal cribbing would appear to have the "edge" (literally) on keystone-shaped corncribs because the square-trimmed slats would form drip points along their lower edges. Wedges could be used in attaching horizontal slats to a straight-sided crib in order to shed rain while triangular slat cribbing was a recommended pattern for the home sawmill. Hinged storm flaps attached to the sides of nineteenth-century cribs were another means of protection from rain.

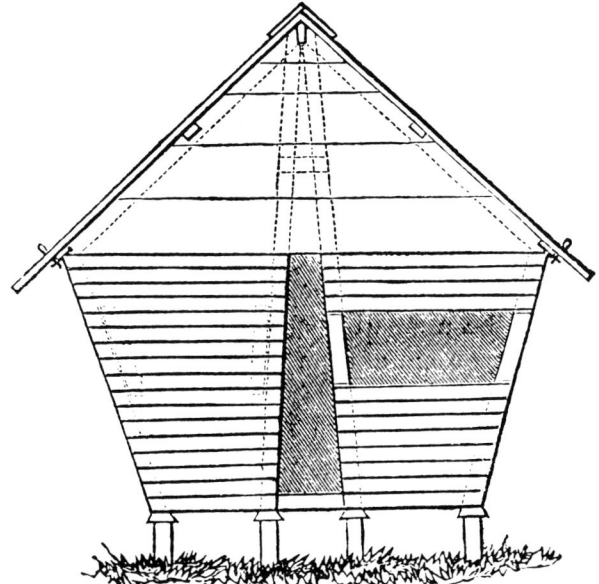

3.13 Connecticut corncrib, common type in the eastern United States. Outward-flaring sides, tin pans over posts, and hinged retractable ladder to help keep out rats and mice. Siding is applied vertically and with very little gap between boards.

3.14 Plan of a corncrib recommended in the pages of the *American Agriculturist*, 1864. In making the center ventilator, a double crib is created.

The rise of commercial sawmills with efficient band saws in the late 1800s gradually replaced the home sawmill as the primary supplier of lumber. This coincided with the timbering of great white pine forests in Michigan, Wisconsin, and Minnesota. Forests of the Great Lakes states provided the lumber for rapidly growing numbers of farmsteads in the prairie-corn states to the south. The cost of building a 1500 bushel "corn house and granary" in 1884 was about $150, including labor of $45, according to an Ohio farmer writing in the *American Agriculturist*.

Commercial saw and planing mills introduced lumber patterns specific to the needs of builders in the last two decades of the nineteenth century. Beveled corncribbing was one such pattern that came into production probably by the 1890s. It may have been produced some years earlier by local mills before the large commercial ones took up the pattern. The edges of beveled cribbing are cut on a slant forming a drip point on the lower edge and a shedding surface on the upper. Usually the boards are spaced about an inch apart on a crib but sometimes they are spaced much closer — tight enough for a kernel of corn to get wedged between. Beveled cribbing made the easier-to-build, straight-sided corncrib more efficient while lessening the value of outward-slanted sides. Even so, the keystone-shaped "corn house" continued to be built by smaller corn producers and home-sawn boards from poplar, tamarack, or cottonwood were often used on these.

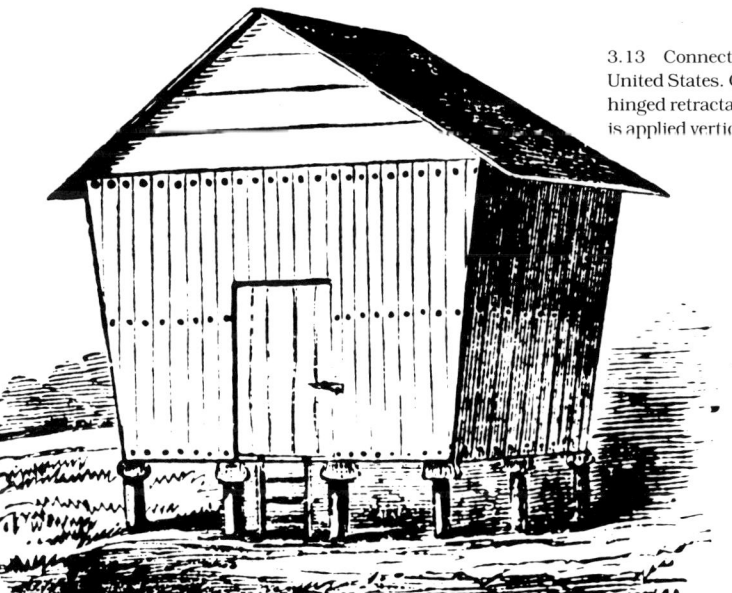

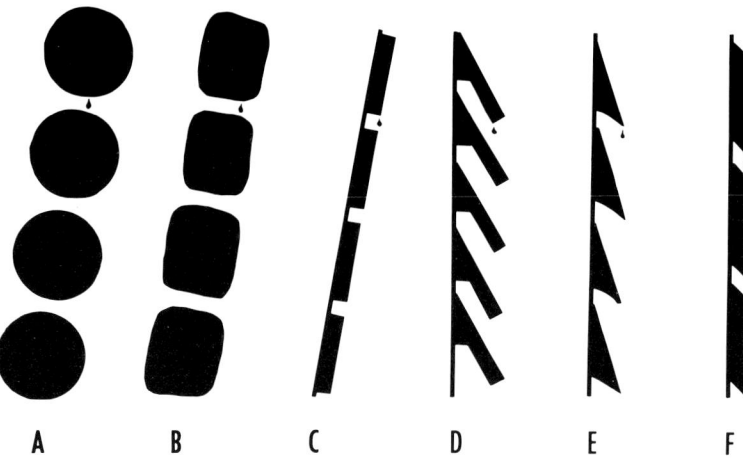

3.15 Rain shedding properties of corncrib walls made from logs or frame and horizontal slats (not drawn to scale). A to C illustrate slanted walls of keystone design. D to F show how straight walls can repel water. *A* round logs. *B* hewn logs. *C* 1- by 4-inch slats. *D* slats on wedges. *E* triangular slats cut from two-by-fours. *F* 6-inch beveled cribbing. The slant illustrated here is 10 degrees. Actually, Scandinavian hayshreds slant outward between 10 and 30 degrees while American keystone cribs average only 5 to 8 degrees.

3.18 Old beveled cribbing spaced wide apart. Wire mesh inside keeps vermin out. Centre County, Pennsylvania, 1982.

3.16–3.17 Late nineteenth century corncrib on the Shirley Plantation, Charles City County, Virginia, 1983. Overlapping board cribbing is attached to wedges along studdings, making it slant outward to shed rain.

Corncribs changed little during their first two and one-half centuries of existence because harvesting methods remained unchanged and mechanization was hardly a factor. Cribs did become more numerous as farms grew in size and as productivity rose during the 1880s. Still they remained only as high as a man could scoop corn from a wagon. Large corncribs were unnecessary on most farms because of relatively small-scale production and because corn was often left in the field in shocks to be gradually husked out as needed.

At least by the mid–nineteenth century both V-shaped and straight-sided corncribs were modified to form the double crib by adding a roof between two single cribs. The driveway or alley formed by this double crib shed (also called a corn shed, corn barn, or corn house in addition to the more familiar double crib) provided shelter from rain or sun while scooping corn into the cribs. It could be used as an animal shelter, for shelling, storage of unhusked corn or farm wagons and, eventually, for machinery. Often a floor was laid over the tops of the cribs at the plate line to form a loft under the roof. This space could be used to store seed corn or other grain and was the predecessor of much larger overhead granaries found in corncribs of the twentieth century. In the Corn Belt the double crib shed prevailed by 1900.

3.20 Rough-sawn native wood cribbing used on slanted wall of crib-shed–granary-garage, built about 1920. Isanti County, Minnesota, 1983.

3.19 George Thompson family, Halcyon, Wisconsin, 1892 to 1894, in classic pose for the camera including canary cage in doorway. Keystone corncrib with sawn board cribbing.

3.21 Double crib formed by roofing over two single cribs.

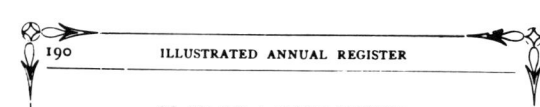

3.22 Early type of double crib with overhead loft for granary.

3.23 Double crib, 19 by 32 feet, with loft, probably built before 1900. Rough 1 by 5 inch board siding attached with square nails. Sherburne County, Minnesota.

A possible earlier description of a double corncrib is found in the diary of Landon Carter whose plantation lay adjacent to Williamsburg, Virginia. An entry of 1771 reads: "I have ordered the Sows between the two Corn house a tight warm snug place...." He also mentions a "60 foot double Shedded house," possibly referring to a corncrib or barn combination.

These first double cribs often retained the V-shape of their predecessors. The sloped walls were supposed to keep the corn from compacting and offer better ventilation and easier unloading—supposedly the corn would roll out. Sometimes only the outer sides were tapered while the inner driveway walls were straight. This was easier to build and gave more unobstructed space in the alley. Equally or more common, however, was the double crib with both inside and outer walls tapered. The single crib may also have only one side flared out. Perhaps some of these were meant eventually to be half of a double crib but for the most part the one vertical side merely provides for easier scooping into the crib. An unusual double crib design has the flare at the gable ends, not the sides, resembling Scandinavian haysheds that have all four sides flared outward.

3.24 Old style double crib covered with mixed sizes of boards and slats. Original scooping doors still have strap hinges. Metal roof and three hatches for elevator are more recent. Centre County, Pennsylvania, 1983.

3.26 Double crib with nearly straight inside walls. Sauk County, Wisconsin, 1982.

One possible incentive for building double cribs was the practice of tenant farming on shares, the corn crop being divided equally between landlord and renter. Matching cribs could more easily be filled equally than could one long single crib.

Tenancy was important in the eighteenth and nineteenth centuries even though cheap new land was available on the western frontier. Of course, not all farmers were adventurous enough for such a move or they didn't have cash for the $1.25 per acre. They could, however, be financed by land speculators or later by the land-grant railroads, effectively becoming tenants. The Homestead Act of 1862 came too late for the small Midwest farmer. Already middlemen had acquired the land, raised the cost to settlers, and made tenancy common if not the only alternative for many would-be farmers.

3.25 Double crib with both inside and outside walls flared. Chisago County, Minnesota, 1983.

3.27 Crib with scooping door on straight side makes filling easier. Washington County, Wisconsin, 1983.

3.28 Unusual crib — the side driveway allows flared ends similar to Scandinavian haysheds. Jefferson County, Wisconsin, 1983.

As corn acreage increased to feed a growing Midwest hog and cattle industry the need for harvesting machinery grew along with it. The laborious job of shocking corn originated in the late eighteenth century in the northern states, especially New York and Pennsylvania, where dairy farmers valued the stalks and leaves as winter fodder. The process of shocking varied but most often began by tying four stalks together to form a fairly secure prop against which other stalks, cut from the surrounding area, could be leaned. The whole bundle would be tied to keep it together. Shocks might be "shucked out" in the field and the ears brought to the crib or the husks might be left attached until removed at a husking bee.

Blade–type corn harvesters and the binder-shocker helped eliminate some hand labor by the 1890s, but still shocking took three times the labor of hand picking and six times that of the future corn picker. Husking corn by hand directly from the row was most common in the corn states such as Illinois and Iowa by 1870 and would remain so until the 1940s.

Introduction of the silo in 1875 delayed the need for larger cribs in many northern areas. Even in the developing Corn Belt, storage of part of the crop as ensilage was a significant factor on many farms until the trend to specialization in cash grain production in the mid–twentieth century.

3.29 Shocking in Lycoming County, Pennsylvania, 1943.

3.30 Husking corn from shock.

Three hundred years after Europeans settled along the East Coast of America in the early 1600s, the harvest and cribbing of corn was still very much a job to be done by hand. Adequate machines for harvesting corn came later than did those for wheat, in part because the corn plant is simply bigger and tougher to deal with but also because equipment capable of doing the job could not be effectively horse drawn. Then, too, the smaller size of the average cornfield compared with those of wheat in the Plains states around the turn of the century made steam power less practical. The need for corn harvesting machinery was less critical than that for small grains because corn could be stored where it grew and husked out as needed to feed on the farm. Not until the mid–twentieth century, when corn had become an important export crop, did the need for large-scale corn harvesting equipment compare with that for other major cash crops.

In the meantime hand picking became a skilled and efficient art, an institution of the Corn Belt, lasting until well after the husking peg and hook were considered antiques by most farmers. Competitions and exhibitions were held annually at fairs and county, state, and national husking contests to determine the champion corn picker.

In the 1930s the national event drew crowds of thousands, coverage by NBC radio, and even the Goodyear blimp. Champions were determined in eighty minutes of furious picking, some contestants at times tossing almost 50 ears per minute into their wagons. Based on an eight-hour day, they could pick at the rate of over 200 bushels per day in heavy corn. The average worker could pick an acre of corn in a day from a standing crop or husk an acre of shocks, equivalent to between 60 and 100 bushels depending on the yield per acre. A two-row mechanical picker could harvest fifteen times as much.

3.31–3.32 Mechanical corn binders of the 1890s.

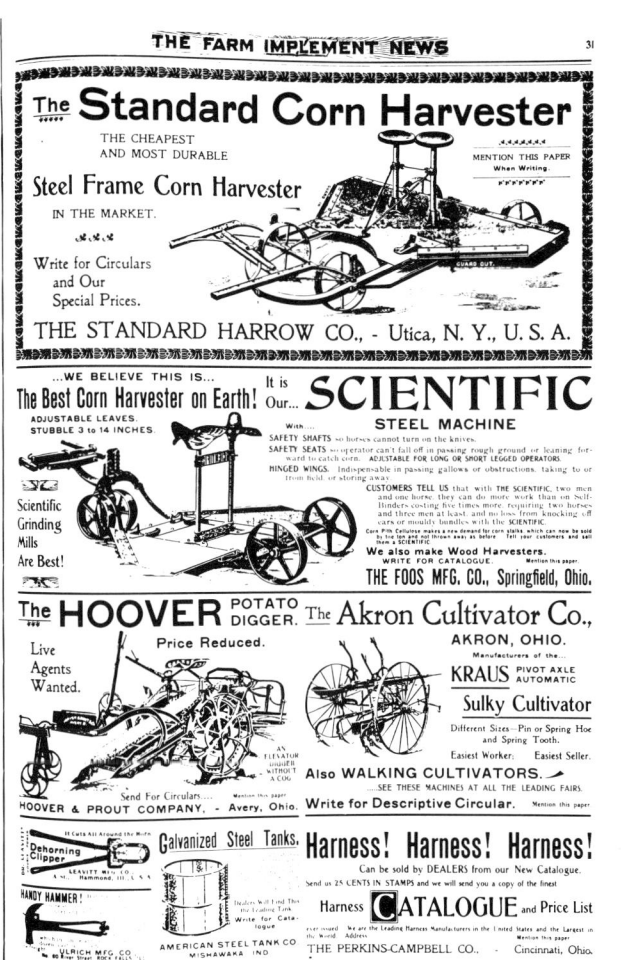

3.33 Blade–type corn harvesters of the 1890s.

3.34 Picking corn by hand, two or three rows at a time, the ears tossed against bangboards. Horses moved ahead on their own in step with pickers.

4

Twentieth Century: Era of Growth

The revolution in American agriculture in the nineteenth century had indeed been dramatic, largely because of massive immigration and the settlement of vast frontier tracts of land. In addition, growing demands for food and feed; access to dispersed markets via rail, canals, and highways; and increased mechanization all stimulated agriculture by the turn of the century. This was to be merely a prelude, however, to agricultural growth in the twentieth century, a story reflected so well by farmstead architecture. Storage buildings that had served for a hundred years with little change would be found inadequate for production in the new century. Scientific and technological advances of the twentieth century resulted in unprecedented growth in agricultural production and mining of the soil, truly a second agricultural revolution.

The twentieth century began with a good economy for agriculture (years later in farm-support programs the federal government's measure of "parity" or a fair price for farm commodities would be based on those prices from 1909 to 1914). Before World War I commodity prices were rising due to rapid urban growth and increased demand for farm exports, which helped the United States meet payments on its foreign debt obligations. The war caused an upheaval in the gradually developing economy. Agriculture expanded rapidly in response to high commodity prices and demands for export to Europe. The United States changed from a debtor to a creditor nation practically overnight. Then, after 1918, with a loss of markets for its great momentum in productivity, came the postwar farm depression.

Since 1920 the twentieth century has been a time of economic ups and downs for agriculture brought on by postwar depression and, after 1933, by a conflict between federal production control/price support programs on the one hand and increased production potential caused by technological developments on the other. The "farm problem" after 1920 has been attributed to overcapitalization of resources in agriculture—that is, too many people engaged in farming and too much investment in equipment and facilities such as storage to be cost effective. The physical plant of agriculture has simply been too productive for its own good. The cost-price squeeze (what farmers pay for their needs versus what they get for the commodities they produce) forced many farmers out of business and into industry or other urban jobs after 1920.

Actually, the percentage of the U.S. population employed in agriculture has decreased steadily since the first census of 1790 when 95 percent of the population was rural. By 1940 this was reduced to 21 percent and by 1960 to only 9 percent. This trend illustrates the constantly growing per capita productivity of farmers, a radical change from subsistence to a complex market economy of cash and credit.

The trend to fewer but larger farms, which began with the agricultural depression in 1920, has been continuous except for the 1930s when farm credit programs encouraged people to stay on the land. American agriculture has fueled its own economic ups and downs as productivity has increased faster than the rate of attrition in farm numbers. Much of this increase in productivity and the trend to larger farms has been stimulated by scientific and technological developments and government farm programs of the twentieth century.

The transformation of farming from a labor-intensive and fairly self-sufficient activity in 1900 to a machine-based industry of cash-crop farming by the 1930s is well illustrated by corn production, harvest, and storage, especially in the emerging Midwest Corn Belt. Developments in agronomic science and agricultural engineering that occurred after 1900 had a mutual and cumulative effect on corn farming and building needs. These developments, discoveries, and inventions played major roles in making corn the king of American crops and, until the 1960s, corncribs the most notable farmstead buildings in Midwest America.

A list of the major contributors to changes in corn farming after 1900 include the gasoline tractor, power–driven corn picker, hybrid seed, commercial fertilizers, portable grain elevator, rubber-treaded tires, and wartime demands for food and crop exports. Additional factors that directly influenced construction of corncribs were federal crop production and storage programs and, until midcentury, relatively inexpensive construction lumber. It is remarkable in a way that some of the greatest stimuli to agricultural production occurred during times of economic depression and severe drought in the 1920s and 1930s.

Hybrid Corn

In 1900 Mendel's "laws of inheritance" were rediscovered, ushering in the age of genetics that would revolutionize corn breeding within two decades. Hybridization of corn had been tried a century before in the early 1800s by John Lorain of Germantown (now part of Philadelphia), Pennsylvania, who developed an improved dent corn by interplanting selected white and yellow kernel varieties. And the famous Reid Yellow Dent, a corn popular in the Midwest around the turn of the century and one of the strains used in modern hybrids, had originated in 1846 by crossing Hopkins Red, a gourdseed type, with Little Yellow, an Illinois flint corn. Such varietal crosses were recommended as a means of increasing yield even in the early 1900s. By 1918, however, hybrid seed was being produced experimentally, with an understanding of the basis for its hybrid vigor, or heterosis as George Shull had named it in 1914. Increased knowledge of the mechanisms of genetics led to greater predictability of success in producing the new double-cross hybrids. Comparatively little hybrid seed corn was produced in the first two decades of the twentieth century, however, and most of that was adapted to eastern climates. The first hybrid available to New England farmers was a Burr-Leaming double cross developed at the Connecticut Agricultural Experiment Station in 1920 by Donald F. Jones. Shull and Jones are credited with developing the methods of plant breeding that led to commercial production of hybrid seed corn. The notion that farmers would make the appropriate crosses of inbred lines to grow their own hybrid seed was advocated for a short time but this proved impractical.

Not until 1926 was hybrid seed corn promoted on a commercial basis. In that year Henry A. Wallace, later secretary of agriculture and vice president under Franklin Roosevelt, formed the Hybrid Corn Company in Des Moines. He had 200 bushels of seed available in 1926 and operated at a loss of $1000. A $33 profit was turned in 1927, $7269 in 1928, and the company was on its way. In 1935 this family concern became the Pioneer Hi-Bred Corn Company. Acceptance of hybrid seed corn was slow at first. In 1929 there were still no hybrids on the "recommended list" of Iowa State College. Markets were depressed and farmers were reluctant to buy seed to produce a crop with decreasing value. Yields might be 20 percent higher than with open-pollinated varieties but why buy seed when you could save your own from familiar fields? The answer came in the drought years of 1933 to 1936 when only the hybrid corn produced any crop at all. Farmers were convinced, more seed companies came into being, and by 1942 in some Corn Belt states up to 98 percent of the corn planted was hybrid. By 1950 the conversion was practically complete for the entire region.

4.1 Open-pollinated–seed-corn ears, selected for quality while picking, are hung under the eaves to dry. Notice that both wagon boxes are placed "backwards" on their running gears. Their tailgates, hinged at the bottom to become scoop boards when let down, are at the front. This indicates that a "right-pitching" scooper is planning to unload these wagons. A "left-pitching" scooper would have the boxes reversed. It would not be possible to simply approach the crib filling door from whichever direction is appropriate to the scooper because the bangboard would be in the way. The lady in this picture is dressed for the camera, not the cornfield. According to her son who took this picture, she wore overalls while picking corn just like her husband. Hamilton County, Iowa, about 1914.

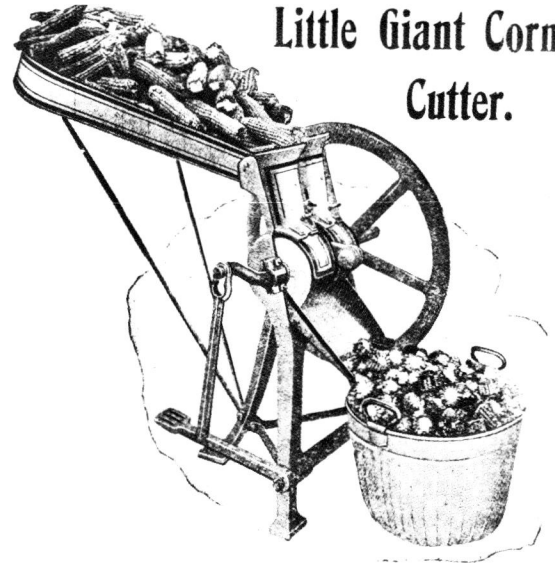

4.2 The gadget just to the left rear of the crib above is a "Little Giant" corn cutter which broke up the ears into three or four pieces for livestock feed.

became important corn-producing regions instead of marginal ones. After 1950 the Great Lakes states showed the greatest increase in acreage and yield; both had nearly doubled by 1962.

Another factor contributing to expansion of the available productive land acreage for corn was land drainage in the wet prairies. This was a gradual development that began on a large scale in the 1870s in Illinois and peaked in Iowa well after 1900. Drainage laws and controversy went hand in hand but the result was vast stretches of rich though low-lying ground made available for corn. Unfortunately, in the zeal to drain every wet spot in the Corn Belt for profit, some marshes and shallow lakes totally unsuitable for cultivation were lost as natural reservoirs and preserves for native plants, waterfowl, and other wildlife.

Corn Picker

No invention dealing with corn in the first half of the twentieth century had so dramatic an impact on the labor of harvest as the mechanical corn picker. One man with machine could suddenly do what three to five had done by hand; later improved models could do much more. Corn-picking machines had been invented in 1850 and 1870 but neither was successful because they broke down the stalks and shelled too much corn. The first important corn picker patent was issued in 1880 and both the McCormick and Deering companies introduced single-row, horse-drawn, and traction-driven machines in 1904. By 1910 there were an estimated 1000 corn pickers on farms in the United States. These early pickers failed to capture a larger market partly due to their cost but also because the machinery was cumbersome. This type of picker was set in motion by a large drive wheel as it was pulled over the ground and it couldn't be geared fast enough with horse power to handle the tough corn stalks or to effectively husk the ears.

Not only did hybrid corn increase total production of this crop (even as total corn acreage was shrinking), it expanded the area where it could be grown. The Corn Belt was pushed northward by creation of new short-season, quick-maturing hybrids. Between 1940 and 1954, southern Minnesota, South Dakota, Wisconsin, and Michigan

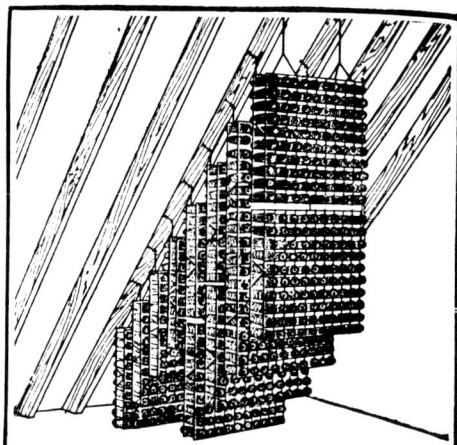

4.3 Some farmers dried seed ears on wires stretched above the crib alley, on nails driven through the rafters, or in seed racks hung out of the reach of rats and mice.

The corn picker had to wait for general availability of the gasoline tractor to become a practical alternative to hand picking. Neither the ponderous steam engines of the 1890s nor the bulky (and balky) kerosene engine tractors such as most Hart-Parr or Rumely models of 1907 to 1923 were adapted to small-farm field work. Their main use was in plowing and belt work such as threshing. It was the small gas tractor that could be hitched to existing horse-drawn machinery that really pushed mechanization. Many such lightweight tractors were manufactured during the prosperity of World War I. For example, the "Bull with the Pull" was produced from 1914 to 1920. It weighed 4650 pounds and cost $645. Henry Ford's Fordson was introduced in 1915, though production didn't really get rolling until 1917. Other small tractors included the Bates Steel Mule, the Kansas City Prairie Dog, and the LaCrosse Happy Farmer. The number of tractor manufacturers peaked at 186 in 1921, just after the beginning of the agricultural depression, and then fell rapidly.

Corn pickers became more available in the teens but still relatively few farmers owned one. In 1913 60 percent of the corn harvest was taken from standing stalks (40 percent from shocks) and nearly all of this was picked by hand. By 1920 about 10,000 farmers had pickers. Even so, $375 in 1923 was a lot to pay for a picker. The real push to mechanical harvest came with development of the tractor power take-off (PTO) in 1924. The first picker-husker for PTO operation, a McCormick-Deering pull type, was sold in 1928. In 1929 two-row, tractor-mounted pickers became available. The PTO provided more adequate speed to run the gathering chains and snapping rollers compared with ground traction machines. A one-row picker of the early 1930s could harvest an acre per hour while by hand it took a day. Still, as late as 1940 more corn than not was picked by hand and many small farmers didn't fully mechanize their corn harvest until 1950.

4.4 This corn picker of 1907 was horse drawn and traction driven by a single large drive wheel. In practice, four or six horses were needed to pull the machine and wagon. Note open gears and chains, making the corn picker a dangerous machine from its beginning.

4.5 Rumely 15–30 OilPull kerosene tractor pulling an eight-bottom plow about 1915 in central Iowa. Attached to the front wheels and extending forward is a front-end, self-steering device which followed the plow furrow. Each of the eight moldboards had to be raised by the individual levers upon reaching the end of the field so the bulky plow could be turned.

In 1947 the PTO was made constant running, that is independent of the clutch being engaged. This meant the picker chains and snapping rollers could be kept running while at a standstill. It also meant the machine became more dangerous. An operator could now leave the seat while the picker ran in order to clear snapping and husking rollers that tended to clog in damp or weedy conditions. Many farmers lost fingers, hands, arms, and legs to pickers in the 1950s. Vigorous safety campaigns were conducted, reverse gears were added to help clear debris automatically, and finally a redesign of the snapping mechanism placed the dangerous rollers beneath a set of protective snapping bars.

Another development that spurred adoption of tractor-mounted or pulled machinery was the low–pressure rubber tire, introduced in 1932, which quickly replaced the heavy steel-lugged wheels. Tractors could move faster on rubber and they caused less soil compaction. Farmers who hadn't turned to rubber tires in the 1930s, however, might find themselves on lugs until 1945 because of wartime shortages and rationing.

4.6 Traction-driven McCormick corn picker pulled by a Bull gas tractor. The three-wheeled "Bull with the Pull" was one of the many popular tractors for small farms produced during the war years. Central Iowa, about 1915.

4.7 A selling point for the small gas or kerosene tractor was that it could be used like a team of horses on implements already owned by the farmer. Special remote control devices allowed a single operator to run both tractor and implement while seated on the latter where adjustment levers were located. This saved the cost of additional help.

There were many difficulties encountered in perfecting the corn picker and these delayed its complete dominance over hand picking. Early pickers had a tendency to shell too much and not recover the grain, not husk well enough (especially compared with good hand picking), and not pick up broken or blown over stalks. There was also difficulty in picking ears at different heights on the stalks. Both the equipment and the corn were modified to make the new laborsaving technology work. The snapping rollers were strengthened and made smaller to shell less corn. The increased strength of stalks and roots of hybrid corn made corn pickers really practical. Corn breeders developed hybrids that would husk more easily and bear uniform-sized ears at a consistent height to match the capabilities of the corn picker. This is in stark contrast to some of the old open-pollinated varieties in which great height and multiple ears were promoted as virtues. For example, an advertisement of 1912 from the Luther Burbank Society proudly announced this famed horticulturist's recent development of corn 16 feet tall with up to 32 ears per stalk. Whether this California creation ever found its way to Illinois or got lost in the tall corn of Iowa is uncertain — and perhaps best left to tall-story tellers. Ironically corn improvement is now so attuned to current mechanization that recent high-yielding but later-maturing varieties are adapted only to combine harvesting. They do not husk well by the "outmoded" corn picker and they tend to shell easily.

Portable Grain Elevator

Before 1910 the height of corncribs was limited by the height a man could scoop. Invention and availability of the portable grain elevator made scooping corn from the wagon a thing of the past and paved the way for much higher corncribs. The first conveyer had been built for a grain elevator in New York in 1848, but corn production didn't reach sufficient levels to create a market for such a machine on farms until the 1890s. Portable grain elevators were widely advertised by 1904 though they were rare on farms even ten years later. Their real development occurred after World War I and it wasn't until 1934 that they were sold in significant numbers. Large corncribs, which required elevators to fill them, were built in the 1920s and earlier but these often used permanent inside cup elevators.

4.8 This tractor, a Farmall F-12, was very popular on the average farm between 1932 and the 1940s. Note the steel-lugged wheels. This farmer hadn't converted to rubber tires yet. The elevator is made of wood (probably cypress), not unusual for its day. The exposed tumbling rod turned fast under tractor power and was dangerous, especially to someone wearing loose clothing. Once a cuff got wrapped around the rod it took only seconds to peel every stitch from one's body and sometimes break bones or dismember. The octagonal corncrib is common yet today and one of the few manufactured of wood.

SCHROEDER'S PORTABLE GRAIN DUMP

Handles 15 Bushels Ear Corn per Minute
It is a Seller and a Winner.

With nine years of experience in this line, we have learned that a machine well built, strong and reliable, needs the least repairs and brings the best results. Write for circulars and prices.

SCHROEDER BROS.
Patentees and Manufacturers   MINIER, ILL.

4.9   This 1904 advertisement shows a portable elevator run by a "horsepower" that also ran the grain dump (wagon hoist or lift).

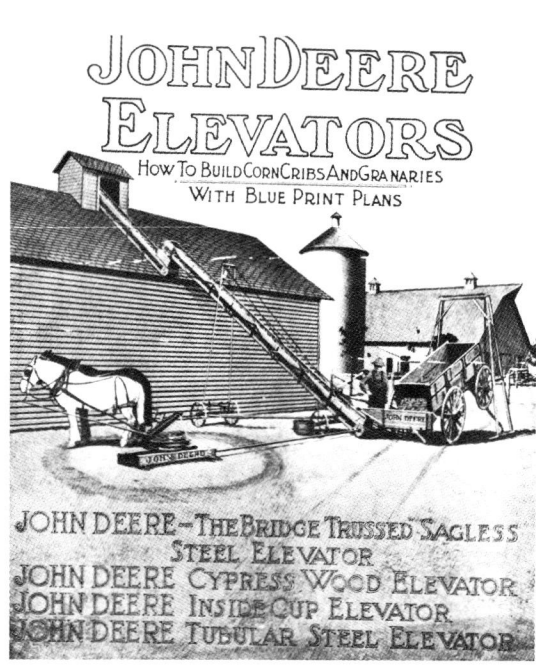

4.10   John Deere brochure of 1916 showing an elevator with roof extension, horsepower, and derrick truck or hoist.

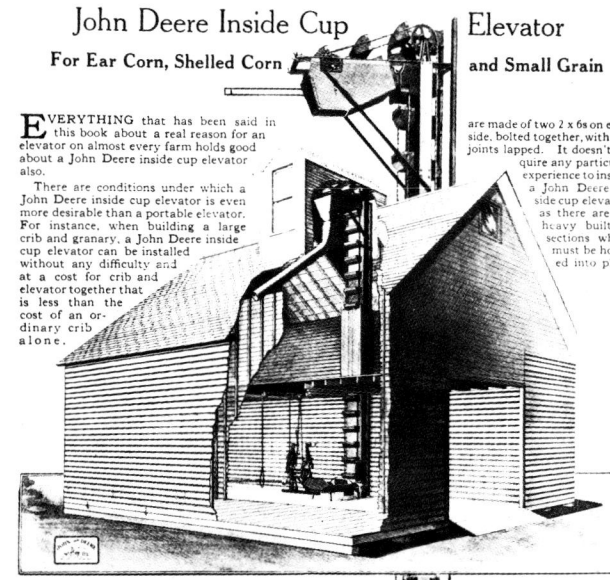

4.11   John Deere brochure of 1916 showing an inside cup elevator installed, with enlargement of hopper mechanism and head section found in the cupola.

4.12 Filling a corncrib by elevator in the early years of using this implement (about 1910), through the existing scooping doors in the alley. Gable end bracing and siding had to be removed to allow the elevator inside. This elevator would not have been long enough to reach the peak of the long flat roof by laying it on the outside. Small box on side of wagon holds husking gloves and seed ears chosen while picking. The hinged bottom part of the end gate has been removed to empty the wagon. The horse that pulled this wagon was left attached during the unloading and its rear is being hoisted off the ground.

4.13 Here an elevator is long enough to reach the peak of the roof. A cupola to cover the elevator head did not yet exist on this crib, formerly filled by hand. Farm machinery was dangerous even in the days of slow-moving horsepowers. Shortly after this picture was taken the woman (again dressed for the camera, not the occasion) lost parts of the fingers on one hand in the chains and gears under the hopper while cleaning up shelled corn. Hamilton County, Iowa, about 1915. The print is from a broken glass plate negative.

Fertilizers

Maintaining soil fertility with manures and fertilizers was not a general practice among the early settlers. Because livestock roamed free and crops were fenced in, there was little recycling of nutrients. By the 1640s, however, some farmers were manuring their fields and in the 1680s Pennsylvania German immigrants were bringing sound values of husbandry to their lands. Still, most farming was in reality mining the soil. Pioneer farming had been based upon breaking new ground and exploiting the soil organic matter and minerals stored up over many centuries in the forest litter or prairie sod. Efficient recovery and use of livestock manures and cropping with nitrogen-fixing legumes gradually became more widely adopted in the nineteenth century.

Mineral fertilizers and soil buffers such as lime or gypsum were available in some areas from natural deposits. Liming of acid soils had been practiced since colonial days—early American farmers used oyster shells from heaps left by Indians as a substitute for the British marl used back home. Potassium was obtained from wood ashes in the early days while along the western frontier in the 1860s buffalo bones were ground up as a source of phosphorus.

The commercial fertilizer industry was founded in England in 1843 with the making of superphosphate. In nineteenth-century America chemical fertilizers were promoted as a new way to replenish worn-out soils, especially those long under cultivation. Unfortunately, most of the early fertilizers were of low analysis (1-8-2, that is, 1 percent nitrogen, 8 percent phosphorus, 2 percent potassium, was a common formulation even in 1902). Furthermore, many were of questionable value at best, sold by unscrupulous salesmen or companies. Fraud was too easy in a business where results weren't measured until after the harvest season. A writer in 1907 compared elements of the fertilizer trade with the patent medicine business.

As early as the 1870s some states began enacting fertilizer inspection laws aimed at eliminating fraud and regulating the industry by impartial testing and labelling. State chemists were to be arbiters between manufacturers and farmers, yet controversy over analyses of content and nutrient values of fertilizers persisted. The need was clear for scientific testing and experimental application of fertilizers on different soils. This was a prime stimulus for creation of several state agricultural experiment stations leading, in turn, to enactment of a national system of experiment stations in 1887.

Fertilizer technology saw its real development in the twentieth century based on growing chemical and munitions industries and cheap petroleum-based energy for production. Not only did the tonnage of chemical fertilizers applied by farmers increase tenfold between 1900 and 1962, but the nutrient analysis likewise rose dramatically in the same time span, averaging 14-11-9 by 1962. Though their long-term effects on the soil itself would prove to be adverse under intensive farming methods, chemical fertilizers did add significantly to corn yields by supporting double or more the stand of plants on the same ground. Adequate rainfall became even more critical under such heavy cropping.

Because of their cost, commercial fertilizers were initially regarded as supplements to animal manures but by midcentury they became substitutes, especially as farmers turned to purely cash-crop production while shifting away from general grain-livestock operations. Development and increased use of nitrogen fertilizers has been especially dramatic beginning with the synthesis of urea in 1935, increased production of ammonium nitrate (for agriculture in addition to explosives) in the 1940s, and especially anhydrous ammonia in 1945. Before 1946 less than 1 pound of nitrogen was used on the average acre of Iowa corn. This would grow to over 80 pounds in 1965. Yet even as late as 1959, some 37 percent of farmers in the United States applied no fertilizer to their crops. The greatest decrease in the price of nitrogen in the form of anhydrous ammonia came after 1960 and the next decade witnessed a great increase in its use. The trend in lower cost was shattered by the oil embargo of 1973.

Government Farm Programs

Controversial and fired with political side taking, farm programs of the United States Department of Agriculture (USDA) have been viewed either as attempts to harness free enterprise or to provide farmers with a fair share of America's prosperity, depending on one's perspective. Other opinions abound, some less kind. In any case, the roller-coaster economic upheavals of the farm sector since World War I are due in part to attempted production controls by government on the one hand and too-productive farmers lacking any control over the prices they receive for their commodities on the other.

The Agricultural Adjustment Act of 1933 was a reaction to the general economic depression and farm distress in the nation. Corn prices were low and hogs sold for the lowest prices in fifty years, if they sold at all. Part of the overproduction of corn in the postwar 1920s was due to the tractor replacing animal power. Between 1918 and 1930 mechanization released some 15 to 25 million acres from feed production. Loss of 10 to 11 million horses and mules reduced the market for corn alone by 15 million acres while at the same time bringing substantial acreage into corn production that formerly produced oats for these draft animals. Most of the excess corn went into hog production. Farmers were caught in a technological-economic double bind. Whereas before the day of the tractor they had been fairly self-sufficient with fuels, they now had to have cash for petroleum but their commodities were worth next to nothing in the marketplace. Without cash or credit, many farmers lost their land.

The objective in 1933 was to reduce production to within market demands. There had been too much corn feeding too many hogs making too much pork for a market with prices too low for producer and too high for consumers faced with economic depression. But regulating production was a state concern according to the Supreme Court and the act was declared unconstitutional. By 1938 Congress had enacted most of the provisions of the earlier act. The Agricultural Adjustment Administration (AAA) of 1938 had as an additional goal the protection of consumers by maintenance of adequate reserves of food and feed. Systematic storage of crops, which became the security for government price-support loans, was the basis for the Department of Agriculture's Ever-Normal Granary plan. This was dubbed by some "Wallace's granary" or his "Joseph plan" after the familiar biblical story. The Commodity Credit Corporation, established in 1933, was responsible for the loans on farm products. When market prices fell below the federally guaranteed loan price, farmers turned over the collateral, the grain itself, to the government.

While controlling the acreage planted to corn might be regarded as successful, the real aim of controlling total production failed. This was due primarily to the greater yields per acre offered by hybrid corn but also because of more intensive farming and use of fertilizers.

One major impact of the grain reserve programs was to stimulate on-farm storage needs and thus construction of corncribs and granaries. Agricultural engineers of the USDA and land-grant colleges experimented with various crib designs to determine how to best provide for corn storage in the Ever-Normal Granary. Federal loans on "sealed corn" paid for many corncribs in the Midwest from 1939 through the 1950s, even into the 1960s. Sometimes corn stayed cribbed for two to five years and, though corn provides its own natural storehouse on the ear, after such lengthy storage much of the grain shelled from these cribs was spoiled by mold, insects, rodents, or simply deterioration. Waste of excess, so to speak.

4.14   Farm foreclosure sale, Denison, Iowa, 1933. National Guard was called in when protesting crowd got out of hand.

4.15 Seventeen-hundred-bushel crib in Harrison County, Iowa, placed under seal of Ever-Normal Granary.

Era of Growth

Though many large old cribs predate the 1920s, the real growth in their size and numbers was between the 1930s and the mid-1960s in response to increased production. Wooden corncribs measuring 27 feet wide by 32 to 40 feet long and holding 3000 to 5000 bushels of ear corn typified the Corn Belt. Some were built much larger — 60 feet or more long with cribs 10 feet wide and 18 feet high holding over 10,000 bushels. A corncrib reported in 1940 to be the largest in Iowa measured 300 feet long and held about 24,000 bushels. The large masonry cribs described later in this chapter held up to 25,000 bushels or more.

4.16 Three corncribs on rails are experimental types being tested at the USDA field station, Urbana, Illinois, for use in the Ever-Normal Granary program. Crib on right has forced air ventilation, crib in center has rain flaps much like those on some keystone corncribs of pioneer days.

If the corncribs on farms were growing to meet the "demands of supply," those at the railheads were sometimes even bigger. Most grain elevators in the 1930s and 1940s had a corncrib attached or nearby to handle the overflow of harvest, to store the crop until dry enough to shell, or to grind ear corn for feed. Some of these cribs were of ordinary size but in the Corn Belt at least a few were massive. One at Matoon, Illinois, measured 100 feet long, 24 feet wide and 35 feet to the eaves of the roof. The structure was formed of two individual cribs 10 feet wide separated by a 4 foot ventilator. Total capacity was 50,000 bushels. To withstand the tremendous pressures in such deep bins, each crib was divided into five 7 foot high frameworks or "bents" tied together with 2 by 10 inch joists. Even with this support it was questioned at the time it was built whether the structure could withstand the great side pressures.

4.17 Laboratory model of a crib designed at Iowa State College. Note unobstructed interior due to gothic roof. Cribs could be filled nearly to top of granary. The grain bins are unusual in having their walls sloped, which allows more space for ear corn. Cribbing in alley is attached diagonally for better bracing.

4.18 Wire mesh and perforated galvanized steel corncribs under test at the Agricultural Engineering Research Farm, Iowa State College, Ames, 1939.

48 TWENTIETH CENTURY

Taken together the scientific discoveries, inventions, world events, and government programs of the twentieth century had a dramatic effect on American agriculture and farmstead architecture. Corncribs in particular reflect the growth of Midwest farm productivity to just beyond midcentury. Growing in size and number they reached their peak of development during crop surplus years in the last three decades of their era. Building corncribs of wood then suddenly became an extinct activity because of changing harvest and storage technologies and greater lumber costs compared with steel.

4.21 A corncrib from Fremont County, Iowa, labelled "largest in the state" in this 1940 USDA photograph. It measured 300 feet long, 14 feet to the peak. The 8-foot cribs were 12 feet high and together held about 24,000 bushels.

4.19 Characteristic size of midwestern corncribs during their era of growth is seen on this farmstead. Hamilton County, Iowa, 1983.

4.20 Large gambrel-roofed corncrib built in 1958, used only a few years for ear corn before being abandoned until the crop surplus of 1986. Sixty-four-feet long with cribs 10 feet wide by 18 feet high, each side held 6000 bushels. The structure was filled by a central inside elevator having conveyers extending laterally from the cupola to spouting which dropped the corn into the side cribs. Hamilton County, Iowa, 1983.

Some regions growing large amounts of corn today never had many corncribs, of course, because the crop is a recent adoption in these areas. Such regions have missed the corncrib era altogether through the introduction of new hybrid varieties, sprinkler irrigation, or other factors that have made corn a more broadly competitive crop since the 1960s. Steel bins and drying systems didn't replace the corncrib here but instead came with the crop.

Changing Harvest Technology

Mechanization finally caught up with the corn crop in 1954 when the corn head attachment for the John Deere combine became available. Other manufacturers quickly followed suit. There had been earlier attempts at producing a corn combine, the first in Queensland, Australia, from 1921 to 1924. The drier climate compared with that of the American Corn Belt made field shelling there possible without subsequent artificial drying. In the United States the Gleaner corn combine of 1930 had failed because of the Great Depression, and the Allis Chalmers corn head attachment for their ALL-CROP Harvester, first produced in 1936, was discontinued in 1941 because of war restrictions.

The combine with corn head was practical in the 1950s and 1960s because of the low cost of fuel to run the artificial dryers, which reduced the moisture content of the shelled corn to safe levels for bin storage. What had been done by air drying of ear corn in cribs over a period of months was now done in days, but at a cost.

While grain lost in harvesting was twice as great with combines (even those of 1968) than with state-of-the-art corn pickers, it was a technology whose time had come. By 1965 more corn was combined than picked and in 1972 two-thirds of the crop was harvested by combine. While only 20 percent of Illinois corn had been field shelled in 1956, by 1980 this figure had grown to 94 percent.

The "picker-sheller" was a contemporary of the combine corn head but it didn't catch on as the latter had. As its name states, it was basically a picker with an attached sheller and bin for storage while on the move. There were pull-types or self-propelled models (the self-propelled corn picker had been introduced in 1946 by Massey-Harris). The picker-sheller was sometimes a cumbersome machine and most lacked the maneuverability, flexibility, and economy of the self-propelled combine with corn head. One homemade, self-propelled, four-row, picker-sheller of 1954 was called a "cornfield battleship." It could harvest 15 to 20 acres in an eight-hour day. A commercial model of the day cost $1935, about twice the cost of the tires alone on some large combines nowadays. Picker-shellers accounted for only 2 percent of the Illinois harvest in 1980, corn pickers 6.5 percent, and the combine with corn head 91.5 percent.

The picker-sheller was invented, or rather assembled, by farmers and implement manufacturers alike. It demonstrates that not all inventiveness has sprung from implement manufacturers and their engineers. Some of the best ideas were generated (and "implemented") by farmers themselves. They did not necessarily wait for commercial production for their machinery needs. The picker-sheller didn't catch on because the combine with corn head was more versatile and efficient but the farmers were ahead of machinery makers in recognizing needs. They were looking for something better — and made it.

4.22 A combine with corn head attachment and behind it another but with small-grain head and reel. Note steel bin with dryer vent at base and auger elevators for shelled grain. To left is a concrete block corncrib with ventilated dome roof of galvanized steel. Sarpy County, Nebraska, 1982.

4.23 The "cornfield battleship," a four-row, picker-sheller assembled by John G. Eyestone, Wyandot County, Ohio, for the 1951 harvest covered 20 acres per day.

The decline in picker harvesting can be seen by comparing the number of manufacturers of chain-type elevators used for ear corn with that of the auger type for shelled corn. In 1949 there were eighty-three companies producing chain elevators while only twenty-two manufactured the auger type. In 1965 there were about ninety of each but by 1970 we find eighty-five manufacturers of the auger type, only thirty-six chain. It became difficult to locate a new chain-type elevator at implement dealers in some areas in the 1970s and, as with the corn picker itself, repairs often became a matter of scavenging parts from a matching model.

The rapid change to field shelling of corn and drying and storing in steel bins eliminated the need for corncribs. High-moisture corn could now be heat dried or, as costs of fuel soared in the 1970s, stored directly in the new airtight Harvestore silos that prevent mold by replacing oxygen with inert gases, such as nitrogen and carbon dioxide. Thus we have come full circle, back to the storage methods of primitive man—in sealed bins or, in his case, in underground pits.

Lumber and Styles

For nearly three hundred years corn production methods had changed little from the pattern of hoeing and husking with horsepower and hand labor of frontier settlers. Storage facilities that had served the pioneer continued to do so until near the end of the nineteenth century or even well into the twentieth when technological advances began to stimulate growth in building size. For approximately the last forty years of its era the corncrib experienced a period of unprecedented growth.

The size and design of corncribs were changing even by the 1870s in response to production and on-farm storage needs. And by 1890 large corn houses existed in the great corn-growing Midwest. One described from Kansas was 100 feet long by 28 feet wide and held 18,000 bushels. While articles in the *American Agriculturist* were still promoting the V-shaped corncrib or Connecticut corn house for eastern farms, the double crib shed was gaining in popularity from Pennsylvania to the expanding Corn Belt.

The geographical distribution of corncribs, their types and styles, is determined by many factors, including the ethnic backgrounds of farmer and carpenter; available lumber supplies; capacity needed for size of crop; promotion and distribution of standard patterns through building services, lumber dealers, and manufacturers; and sales areas of factory-made cribs. Because the corncrib, like other farm buildings, is a practical structure its size reflects production above all else wherever it is found. The largest corncribs are, of course, found in the heart of the Corn Belt.

The wood corncrib is a classic example of folk or vernacular architecture. It has been custom built by farmers or rural carpenters throughout its history (there have been some round or octagonal, wood-slat manufactured cribs but these are the exception that proves the rule).

Rural carpenters learned their trade on the job and copied designs they saw that worked well and were economical of lumber. They settled on a few designs, customized to suit the wishes of clients, and their individual styles can be seen over the one or several counties where they worked. A particular type of cupola or pattern at the eaves might be seen throughout a county or locality due to one builder's influence. Some crib styles are distinctly regional. For example, the long double-cupola cribs of Illinois, each generally with its own elevator. This may be a regionalism in both style and habit of use — the farmer simply finds it more convenient not to move one elevator between cupolas. Sometimes a corncrib is patterned after an existing barn, in roof type or more superficially.

During the heyday of building large wood corncribs around midcentury, the carpenter who specialized in farm buildings was in considerable demand. If corn prospects looked good during the summer many farmers wanted new cribs and they sought out the rural carpenter to build them. He worked much faster than the house builder and usually for lower wages. Spring to fall was the building season and, if the carpenter was also farming, he fit tending his crops between jobs. Carpentry might become nearly a second full-time job for off-the-farm income. In a good summer he could build ten cribs, averaging one every two weeks, with a crew of four to six men.

The farmer/carpenter of the mid–twentieth century carried on traditions established early in this country. The few immigrant carpenters arriving in the original colonies in the seventeenth and early eighteenth centuries expected to carry on their trade but often discovered instead that they had to turn to farming for their livelihoods. There simply wasn't enough substantial construction going on in the villages and the thrifty settlers, scattered as they were, often built their own hovels. These carpenters-turned-farmers advertised their skills to obtain extra income or for exchange work.

Things were rather the reverse by the twentieth century. The postwar depression of the 1920s and 1930s caused some farmers to take up carpentry for extra income. And a good carpenter during the heyday of constructing farm buildings of wood

4.24 Manufactured stave-type, wood-slat crib encircled by steel hoops much like a silo. Behind it is a triple crib. Hamilton County, Iowa, 1983.

4.25 The factory-made, octagonal, wood-slat corncrib is a common sight throughout northern corn growing areas. Some cribs of this design are homemade. Jones County, Iowa, 1981.

didn't have to advertise. His reputation preceded him. He often worked for wages and signed no contract with the farmer — arrangements were by mutual agreement and trust.

In preparation for drawing up the building plan a carpenter needed only to learn what size corncrib the farmer wanted, the desired roof type, and whether it was to have an overhead granary. Using only a small steel square, the carpenter would sketch a simple end view or "bent" of the crib. This was all the blueprint necessary for preparing a material order list and for construction. The plan determined not only the look of the structure because of width, height, and pitch of roof, but also the dimensions of lumber to be used. No detailed blueprints were made or standard building plans used — most cribs were variants of patterns familiar to the carpenter and their construction was based upon experience. A materials list was necessary so the lumberyard manager could cost out that part of the project and ensure availability of all needed materials when construction began.

4.27   Hamilton County, Iowa, 1982.

Designs of individual carpenters mix with styles wanted by farmers to produce an endless variety of vernacular form in the corncrib.

4.26   Hamilton County, Iowa, 1983.

4.28   Washington County, Iowa, 1983.

TWENTIETH CENTURY 53

4.30 Hamilton County, Iowa, 1983. This crib is set at an oblique angle in the farmyard rather than the more typical north-south or east-west orientation. The off-center cupola can be built smaller than a symmetrical one centered on the ridge line and is cheaper because it uses less material. The cupola's main purpose is to accommodate a portable elevator or to cover the head of an inside elevator. Since the latter is built off to one side of the alley, the smaller offset cupola is adequate, though some farmers prefer the looks or greater interior working space offered by a symmetrical one.

4.31 Corncribs with twin cupolas are common in central Illinois. Usually each cupola sports its own elevator, a luxury in equipment perhaps but much easier to work with than having to move a single elevator. Presumably the cribs are too long to be served by one cupola. Henry County, Illinois, 1982.

4.29 Hamilton County, Iowa, 1983.

4.32 Often the farm buildings are matched in paint and trim color. Here as a further gesture to match the crib and barn we see a functionless snout on the crib. Hamilton County, Iowa, 1983.

4.33 This unusual T-shaped corncrib from western Ohio is similar in design to the large barns with side extensions common in the northern part of the state and in Pennsylvania. Practical in its use of a central elevator system, it probably doesn't provide the best ventilation. Paulding County, Ohio, 1985.

The building site for a corncrib was chosen for its ease of access and use by the farmer. In the early years this might have meant a location close to a hog feeding operation but on the mechanized mid–twentieth-century farm a more important factor was ready access for elevators, shellers, trucks, and trailers. A well-drained site was easiest to build on. Low ground was avoided as was too great a slope that would require a large foundation.

Standard farm-building plans and designs were first promoted in agricultural books and magazines of the nineteenth century and were widely distributed in the twentieth century by implement manufacturers, lumber dealers, commercial farm services, and state agricultural schools. Whether these plans had much influence on crib designs is uncertain, partly because they are so like existing structures it is difficult to see who copied whom. An exception may be the use of pole framing in construction. Pole building designs were promoted as cheaper alternatives to all-dimension lumber framing and concrete foundations. The Midwest Farm Plan Service and Doane Building Service, along with lumber manufacturers, were major proponents of this type construction. The pole and wire or pole and snowfence crib became about as ubiquitous as the factory–made, wire-mesh crib.

Self-feeding cribs were popularized in the days of ear corn rations for hogs. These were claimed to be labor savers and efficient pork producers. The Doane "Cribeteria" was a 450 bushel binlike crib set on a platform to keep the feed off the ground. Similar cribs for feeding ear corn to cattle (calfeterias?) had been available in the nineteenth century.

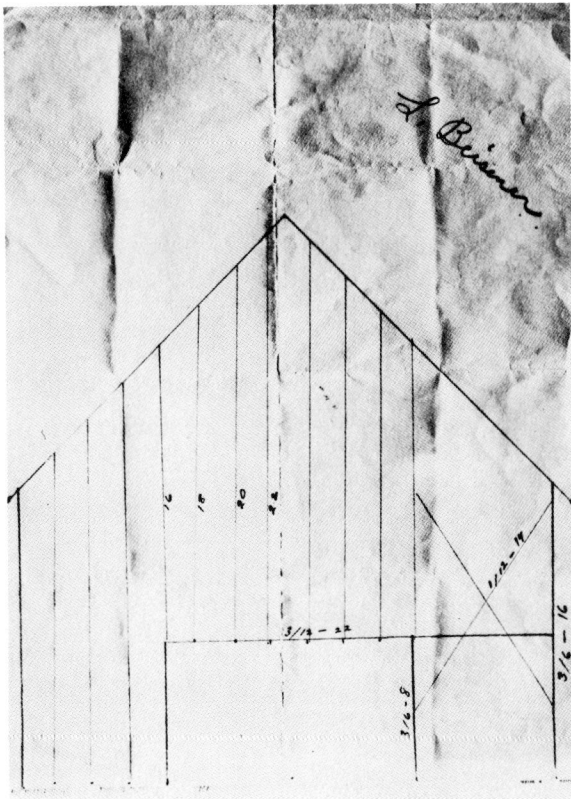

4.34 Building plan, drawn in pencil, consists of an end view ("bent"). With studdings set on 2-foot centers, this structure will have 8-foot cribs and a 13-foot alley. Alleys were of odd measurement because they were spanned by even length (12 or 14 foot) bin joist timbers, allowing 6 inches of overlap to rest on the inside plates at each end.

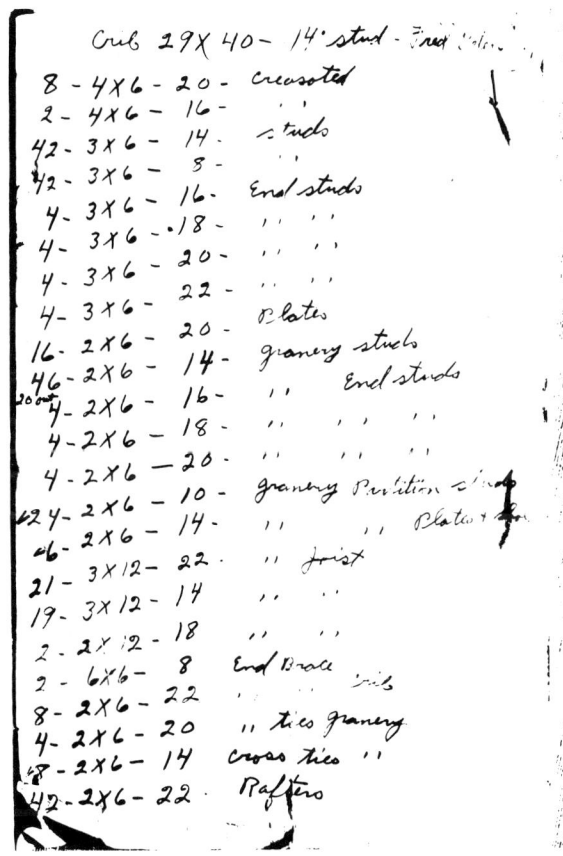

4.35 Material list drawn up in preparation for building an average corncrib. A gable roof is planned with 22-foot rafters. The alley will be 13 feet wide.

4.36 Corncrib adjacent to hog feed lot. Feed close to need was important in the days of mostly hand labor. Ear corn is fed here by tossing it from ramps extending out from doors. Openings in foundation indicate that the hogs are housed beneath the crib, not favorable for drying corn. Tama County, Iowa, 1919.

TWENTIETH CENTURY

4.37 Good location for the corncrib with plenty of open space for shelling. The husks are being burned as they are blown toward the fence. LaSalle County, Illinois, 1983.

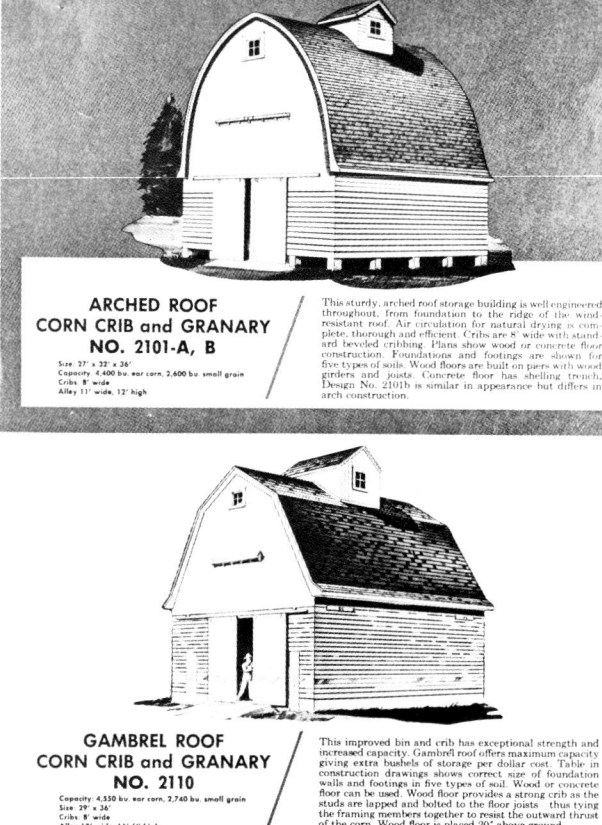

4.38 Corncrib designs from Weyerhaeuser Lumber Company in the 1950s. Detailed construction plans were available to carpenters.

Some frame corncribs built around the turn of the century remain today and may be identified by their slat cribbing of 3 to 5 inch rough boards often cut a full inch thick. Lumber for these cribs frequently came from local timber resources and was cut on home sawmills. Hardwood timber was sometimes the most readily available and a corncrib of solid oak or walnut was not uncommon. One New Jersey crib plan from 1881 recommended 5 by 5 inch oak framing and 3 inch wide oak strips for siding. Cost was $100 for this 16 by 20 foot, 700-bushel crib. A 6000 bushel western corn house of around 1890 was built entirely of native oak and walnut. Not until about 1890 did commercially milled and planed lumber, including patterns such as beveled cribbing, become available in many areas. Being more expensive than home-sawn lumber, such milled and planed patterns were not widely used until the 1920s or 1930s in some areas.

The settlement of the Corn Belt and storage of crops produced from the rich prairie soil relied upon the forests of Minnesota, Wisconsin, and Michigan for lumber supplies beginning about 1856. Vast quantities of logs or unseasoned, rough-sawn timbers were floated down tributaries of the Mississippi to mills at LaCrosse, Dubuque, Davenport, and St. Louis. Water transport was cheaper than rail even when the latter did become available, but it would have damaged finished lumber. Consequently, most northern sawmills until the 1870s produced only rough lumber. Finishing was done at wholesale markets in Chicago, northern Illinois, or railroad towns along the Mississippi.

The growing network of railroads in the Midwest during the last quarter of the nineteenth century allowed direct shipment of lumber from mill to consumer. Before retail "line yards" sprung up along the railroads, lumber was often ordered by mail from wholesale mills. Even in 1918 rural lumber yards rarely had delivery service. Manufactured corncribs, too, such as the metal and wood-slat types could be ordered through catalog retailers.

TWENTIETH CENTURY   57

4.41 The "Cribeteria" for hogs, from Doane Agricultural Service, 1951, a post and snow fence design.

4.39 The post-frame corncrib used 4 by 4-inch pressure-treated posts or poles. The hayshed shown here uses corncribbing for ventilation and to shed water, an irony of function considering that the corncrib may have originated as a modified hayshed.

4.40 Pole or 6 by 6-inch post corncribs use steel mesh or snow fence cribbing and horizontal supports to prevent bulging. Such crib designs were promoted by lumber companies and farm services in the 1950s as economical alternatives to all-wood cribs. Here the slanted bottom aids in emptying the crib. Stearns County, Minnesota, 1983.

4.42 Self-feeding corncrib for cattle. In the 1950s the Midwest Plan Service offered a similar crib of 750 bushels capacity.

4.43 Round wood-slat corncrib. This crib looks much like the common snow fence variety of today but was made of oak slats. It could be ordered from Montgomery Ward and Company in 1898 for $10 to $20 depending upon size.

The retail lumber trade grew out of a need for local, readily available supplies of lumber in small to moderate quantities. The yard manager often had to special-order supplies for larger building projects such as corncribs. Otherwise he might have to scurry around trying to obtain certain required lumber patterns or sizes from other line yards while a carpenter crew waited impatiently in midproject.

Lumber yards today often carry in their inventories many nonconstruction items such as garden supplies or lawn furniture. The farm supply approach seems to have been a tradition in the business. Inventories of small town lumber yards from 1912 to 1914 show them selling bee supplies, buggies, coal, coffins, grain, hair, harnesses, hog troughs, incubators, salt, school desks, and silos among other items besides lumber and associated building materials. Of these only silos, school desks, and hog troughs, in that order, accounted for significant sales.

Large wholesale mills, using efficient band saws and drying kilns, were filling a growing proportion of lumber needs by the early 1900s — over half of total production by 1914. With lumber costs averaging $12.00 per 1000 board feet and carpenters charging $2.50 per day for their skills, a house could be built for $1000.00 in 1901 and an outbuilding such as a corncrib for a fraction of that, say $150.00 to $200.00. By the early twentieth century, too, the great northern white pine forests had been depleted and the lumber industry moved to the Douglas fir forests of the Pacific Northwest or the yellow pine forests of the South.

Both timbers provided more durable construction lumber than white pine and were less brittle, though the harder yellow pine split more than fir and was sometimes excessively resinous to work with. It was evident but ignored at the time that timber was the first of America's great natural resources to be used beyond its limit of replacement or new development.

To be cost effective, rail transport from Washington, Oregon, and California meant shipment of mill-finished lumber. Thinner boards and smaller dimension stock took less space in railroad cars and returned more profit. Consequently, reduced thicknesses of lumber were produced by different companies but there was no uniformity among them. Instead of cutting a full-inch thick, boards were cut and planed to three-quarter inch or thereabouts while two-by-fours became approximately one and a half by three and a half inches in cross section. Using mixed sizes from different companies made construction difficult at best and pointed to the clear need for lumber size and grade standards. The American Lumber Standards were adopted industrywide beginning in 1924 but controversy among lumber manufacturers continued. Standard patterns for millwork such as beveled cribbing were also adopted though minor size differences remained among various brands.

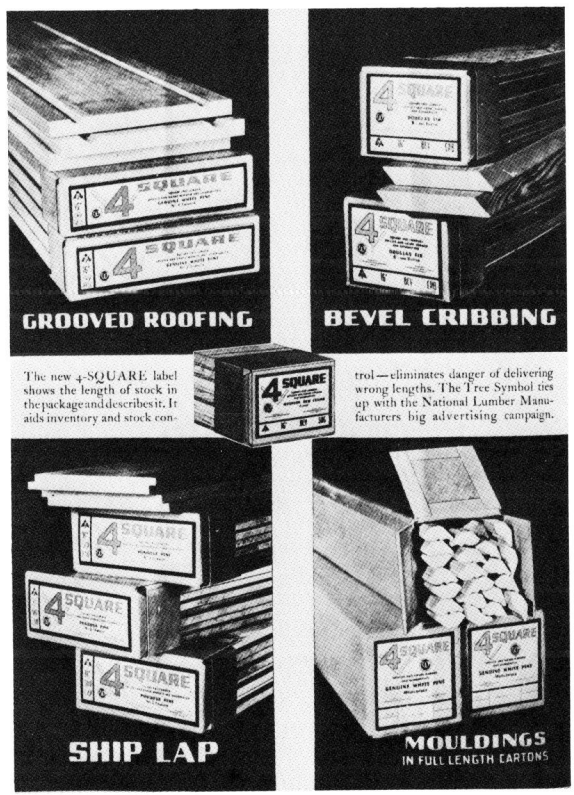

4.44 Wholesale lumber mills sold direct to consumers in the early 1900s before retail "line yards" were widely established.

4.45 Beveled cribbing was one of the standard milled patterns produced by lumber manufacturers since shortly before 1900. In 1928 Weyerhaeuser adopted its "4-Square" policy of consistent lengths and square-cut ends. This made less sawing necessary at the construction site.

Styles and Geography

Construction types and styles often can tell us about our heritage, the ethnic origins of today's human environment. Roof types are especially useful in dating introductions of styles to a region because of their known times of origin.

The simple boxlike single crib with thatch or cornstalk roof served colonial and pioneer homesteaders from the mid-1600s until well into the nineteenth century. Similar cribs have been used in this century. These are often hastily built and meant to be temporary, perhaps holding corn only over winter.

From Appalachia west to Missouri and Texas the unchinked log crib with gable roof was constructed from locally cut timber. It was built as an integral part of a larger barn or as a separate structure until at least 1900 when dimension lumber and sawn boards were becoming more available. Log construction never caught on in the Midwest to the extent it had in the South perhaps because of the abundant softwoods from the Great Lakes states. Settlement came later in the Midwest than in the South and sawmills were more abundant by then. Lumber distribution was also easier along northern waterways and later by rail than along roads in the southern mountains. Some log cribs were built in the Midwest, however, especially by Scandinavian immigrants in Minnesota, Wisconsin, and northern Iowa.

From the Old South, settlers moved westward over the mountains into Kentucky, Tennessee, and southern Ohio after the Revolution to form the earliest Corn Belt and they brought the binlike fence rail, frame and board, or log cribs with them. A simple sloped roof of bark, thatch, or boards was the cover. Sometimes a corncrib was built into the tobacco shed or other barn.

As corn production outgrew the single crib in the developing Corn Belt, double cribs were formed by extending the roof over a pair of cribs to form a gable roof. If the gap between the cribs was then lofted over, extra space was gained beneath the roof for overflow storage of ear corn. Spreading the cribs apart not only increased the loft space but created a storage area below for wagons, tools, and implements. Thus was evolved the double crib shed which became common in the Midwest by 1900. The loft of a double crib shed was used not just as extra space for ear corn but to store hay, seed corn, or bags of grain. Grain bins were soon added and loft joists strengthened in the next stage of evolving the double crib with overhead granary which became the standard of the twentieth-century Corn Belt. Wider alleys offered greater space for machinery storage and are especially seen in cribs lacking overhead granaries. Even here, however, the space was limited compared with a machine shed. Crib alleys were expensive storage.

Barns have always seen multiple use. These have one side or part of a shed devoted to ear corn storage.

4.47   Lancaster County, Pennsylvania, 1983.

4.46   Pole and fence crib with cornstalk thatch cover. Indiana, 1936.

4.48 South Carolina, 1930s.

4.49 Bank barn with crib shed on left. Centre County, Pennsylvania, 1983.

4.50 A pair of single cribs with shared bracing, which makes for a more stable overall structure. A double crib would result if these cribs were joined by a common roof. A double crib shed would result by flooring over the upper cross braces and filling in the gables. Many cribs were built in such pairs to facilitate splitting the crop between tenant and landowner but equally important was structural stability. Both cribs can be filled with one elevator setting, through the upper openings (three seen here). Hamilton County, Iowa, 1982.

Covering a large double crib with a gable roof requires longer rafters than the standard dimension lumber supplied by many yards. Special-ordered–two-by-sixes of 22 to 24 foot length were preferred by carpenters but were also expensive, and some gable roofs were built with two-piece rafters spliced at the purlin plate.

In the heart of the Corn Belt, where greater ear corn capacity was needed and where larger overhead bins for grain storage were desired, the gambrel roof became common in the twentieth century. Most really large cribs are of this type or of Gothic design. The Gothic or round roof was promoted between 1920 and 1950 as prefabricated rafters, made up of glue–laminated 1 by 2 inch wood strips, became available through lumber dealers. The gambrel roof can be made self-supporting (no purlin plate required) and the Gothic roof is always so, thus providing considerable internal space unobstructed by bracing. This is less of an advantage in corncribs than barns, however, because of the need for open haylofts in the latter.

The factory–made Gothic rafter was the only element of a wood crib not normally constructed by the rural carpenter. There were plans available for doing so and some individuals made their own, but generally it was more convenient if not cheaper to use ready-made rafters. Only the ends had to be custom cut at the building site to fit the particular roof pitch selected by the farmer. A crib with Gothic roof was as easy for the carpenter to build as any other, though nailing shingles to the steep lower part felt a bit like leaning backward against the air. A scaffold was often used on this part of the roof in place of mere toeholds.

4.52 The single crib shed. The cribbing used here is actually car siding, a common lumber pattern for exterior shed walls. Centre County, Pennsylvania, 1982.

4.53 Meeker County, Minnesota, 1983.

Two forms of the double crib shed, this one with a separate loft above the alley as seen by the doors in the gable. The loft evolved into an overhead granary.

4.51 Washington County, Virginia, 1974.

4.54 Double crib with overhead granary. Hamilton County, Iowa, 1983.

4.55 Gambrel-roofed crib showing a common way of accommodating a portable elevator so it can reach the peak of a high roof. The three end ties just over the alley help keep the overhead bins from bursting under pressure from grain. Hamilton County, Iowa, 1983.

4.56 Gothic-roofed crib. Hamilton County, 1982.

The great building years for Midwest corncribs occurred between the late 1930s and mid-1960s, well after local or regional softwood lumber supplies were exhausted. Lumber from the Pacific Northwest and southern forests remained relatively inexpensive, however, until past the midcentury mark and kept the large wooden corncrib economically viable. Most cribs during their heyday were custom built by rural carpenters rather than manufactured. By the 1960s this situation was reversed. The new corn-harvest technology combined with higher lumber prices made the wood corncrib both impractical and uneconomical to build. The wire-mesh crib would carry on the tradition of ear corn storage but it was the steel bin for shelled corn that had really come of age.

4.57 Not all Corn Belt cribs are large, as seen by this one under the shade of the old cottonwood tree. Washington County, Iowa, 1983.

4.58 Wire-mesh crib with galvanized steel roof. Hamilton County, Iowa, 1983.

4.59 Large steel-mesh cribs multiply the storage capacity of an old double crib. Iroquois County, Illinois, 1982.

Manufactured Cribs

Wire or welded bar-mesh corncribs like those marketed today became popular after World War II as steel products once again became available for domestic needs. Their popularity grew in the 1950s as lumber and labor costs began to rise. Steel-mesh cribs are easy to fill and empty mechanically, do not sag out of shape, require little maintenance, and hold more than most small single wood cribs. Round or octagonal steel-strap cribs are also common.

4.60 Steel bins and drying equipment almost dwarf the double crib with side extension. Hamilton County, Iowa, 1983.

4.61 Octagonal steel-strap crib, rather common and many still in use. Sauk County, Wisconsin, 1981.

4.62 Round steel-strap crib. Centre County, Pennsylvania, 1981.

Another welded steel-crib design of the early 1950s was made of quarter-inch rods. Rectangular in shape, its walls were strengthened and self-supporting due to their corregated pattern. The crib was relatively expensive but sturdy and most that exist today remain in usable condition. These structures were never as popular as the common wire-mesh or steel-strap cribs and it seems that few were made or sold. They are seen occasionally in Ohio and Iowa.

4.63 The Behlen All Metal Corn Crib, made of steel rods in a corrugated pattern for strength. Putnam County, Ohio, 1981.

4.64 Closer view of wall pattern in above crib.

Earlier types of steel corncribs had been manufactured. From about 1910 to 1941 several companies produced round or rectangular cribs of perforated steel plates or sheets. The galvanized steel corncrib was promoted in advertising during World War I as a means of protecting vital food supplies from rats, fire, and theft. The farmer was supposedly doing his patriotic duty if he bought a steel crib. Restrictions on domestic steel consumption in World War II brought a virtual end to production of metal cribs. The Sears Roebuck catalog listed them as available until 1943, and some are known to have been sold in the 1950s. A surprising number of these cribs exist yet today from Pennsylvania and Ohio to Iowa and Minnesota, though most sit neglected and rusting away. Perforated steel cribs cost more per bushel of storage capacity than did wood cribs, and they did not provide adequate ventilation to allow proper drying of ear corn.

The popcorn crib is a special-purpose structure, a metal-covered, wood-frame crib. Even the inside wooden cribbing is attached over a layer of hardware cloth. The additional protection of the grain from rats and mice is necessary because it is destined for direct human consumption unlike the case with processed corn or feed grain.

4.65 Metal corncribs were promoted during World War I as safe storage for much needed grain.

4.66 Empty and rusting, this steel crib from Union County, Ohio, 1982, has stood for perhaps seventy years.

68 TWENTIETH CENTURY

4.67 Sign on above crib reads: "The Iron Crib & Bin Co., Wooster, Ohio, U.S.A. Sole manufacturer of Fire and Rat Proof Grain Structures and Automobile Houses, under the Marshall Patents. Patented June 29, 1909, other patents pending."

4.68 Perforated steel crib and hand sheller, still in use. McLeod County, Minnesota, 1983.

4.69 Perforated steel-plate crib. Medina County, Ohio, 1981.

4.70 In center is a perforated steel crib of the type marketed between 1910 and 1940, on left a wire-mesh crib, and on right a steel bin. Hamilton County, Iowa, 1981.

4.71 Shelling door of above crib.

4.72 Wood popcorn crib covered with perforated steel siding for extra protection from rats and mice. White County, Indiana, 1982.

4.73 Close-up of shelling door and steel siding of above crib.

Masonry Cribs

Corncribs built of concrete blocks or glazed, hollow clay-tile were sold from about 1910 to the early 1950s primarily in Iowa, Illinois, and eastern Nebraska. Competing with steel-crib manufacturers, the producers of concrete and clay tile advertised their cribs and silos as ratproof, fireproof, long lasting, and practically maintenance free. Clay-tile cribs are especially restricted to those areas having suitable clays for making tile and the few manufacturers who produced them. Because of their weight the clay-tile or concrete blocks could be shipped economically only short distances from the factory and generally over paved roads. Evidence of a crib salesman's activity can be seen today in the clustering of these structures along older improved roads.

Clay-tile corncribs were built in oblong or rectangular shape as well as the round design common to both clay and concrete types. The rectangular tile crib is not uncommon in Iowa. Most such cribs had steel-rod crossties added as support against side pressures of the corn.

Concrete-block cribs held together by encircling steel hoops.

4.74 Two-bin crib. Sarpy County, Nebraska, 1982.

4.75 Four-bin crib. Holding tank for shelled corn along side was used in the drying operation before storage in the steel bin, behind. Wright County, Iowa, 1981.

The concrete or clay blocks were cast with perforations allowing ventilation but supposedly too narrow for rats to gain access. Some concrete blocks had steel bars or wire in the vents to exclude rats. Thus like the steel crib these structures were promoted as rat and fireproof. A feature of clay tile was that its vents sloped downward to the outside allowing better water runoff.

As with steel cribs, the concrete and clay structures were usually erected by a crew employed by the company or local representative selling them. The rural carpenter was usually not involved with the masonry though he might be with the roof or wooden interior bins and vents. A mason, often a silo builder, was called upon for erecting clay-tile cribs as these were mortared together. The real strength of round or oval masonry cribs, though, came from the steel hoops encircling them at intervals of 12 to 24 inches. Cribs of concrete block were usually held together only by these steel hoops and the special, interlocking tongue and groove shape of the stave blocks. The large masonry corncribs are imposing structures with an alleyway between two or four cribs of 12,000 to 25,000 bushels total capacity, one or two inside elevators, and several overhead bins for grain storage.

4.76 Shelling door of this two-bin crib holds steel hoops in place. Frame is made of heavy steel plate to withstand pressures.

72 TWENTIETH CENTURY

Cribs of vitrified clay tile could be round, oblong, or rectangular.

4.77 Two-bin oblong crib with encircling steel hoops. Corn dryer in front to left of alley. Hamilton County, Iowa, 1981.

4.78 This single-bin crib held 18,000 bushels, was easy to fill, but provided poor ventilation due to size. Story County, Iowa, 1981.

4.79 Rectangular crib built on standard design for wood cribs. Ventilating tiles do not extend even to height of alley doors, providing inadequate drying of corn. Crib sides have been reinforced by tie rods. Calhoun County, Iowa, 1982.

4.80 Concrete-block crib with steel rods cast in the ventilation slots that prevent entrance by rats — but not if the door is left open. The blocks in these cribs are made with tongue-and-groove interlocking edges to help hold the structure together. Kossuth County, Iowa, 1983.

4.82 Converted masonry cribs often become part of a complete grain-handling system. Here a four-bin, concrete-block crib has been covered with steel siding. Wright County, Iowa, 1983.

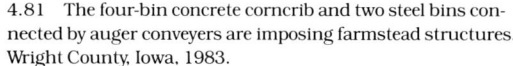

4.81 The four-bin concrete corncrib and two steel bins connected by auger conveyers are imposing farmstead structures. Wright County, Iowa, 1983.

Tile and block cribs did not work out well for ear corn storage. They were often too large for good ventilation and adequate drying of corn (the cribs were sometimes 20 feet in diameter). Also, because of their great height, the corn shelled and compacted badly upon falling as the cribs were filled. Concrete absorbed and held moisture and both types were expensive. Some masonry cribs have been converted to shelled corn storage by covering them with tight-fitted siding but most sit empty today, fossillike behemoths of the Midwest.

Except for local clusters of masonry cribs in the Midwest, most corncribs were built of wood. A survey in 1957 showed that over 86 percent of cribs from four regions of the United States were wood. Metal cribs accounted for only 3 percent and masonry less than 0.3 percent. The rest were combinations of wood and metal or masonry.

Special Crib Designs and Decoration

The American farmer and rural carpenter have modified existing cribs in a variety of ways, built crib-shed combinations, and created some unique designs. They have also expressed a flair for the artistic on occasion. It would be an injustice to overlook such unique or local building designs created out of a natural curiosity, rural inventiveness, or a quest for the ultimate in utility.

Wood and masonry cribs, for example, have been built with the alley running crosswise instead of through the gable ends. This rather common design allows for a greater ear corn capacity, nearly to the peak of the gable. The square crib was supposedly more efficient in use of space and lumber.

Perhaps unique and certainly homemade is the all-concrete corncrib near Mt. Vernon, Iowa. Spurred by a passion to use concrete, Ely West built this crib of his own design in 1927 to 1928 (between 1910 and 1940 concrete buildings such as barns were being promoted by cement associations and tested by agricultural colleges). Measuring 36 feet long and holding 3500 bushels of ear corn with bins for 2600 bushels of grain, the crib stands today hardly changed by time, a tribute in stone to its builder. It is made entirely of concrete except for the inside slat cribbing and, strangely enough, the wood floor which as usual has been undermined by rats. The entire building was formed and poured in place, even the roof and cupola. The side walls and roof were built up in 2-foot sections at a time. Ventilation holes in the sides and ends were provided by laying soaked corn cobs horizontally in the forms as they were filled. Later, upon drying, the cobs were punched out leaving holes every 12 inches. Mr. West also built a garage and a second corncrib of concrete.

4.83 Machine shed, corncrib combinations are common in some areas. Dodge County, Wisconsin, 1982.

4.84 By adding this single crib the farmer could take advantage of the elevator system in the existing double crib. Story County, Iowa, 1983.

4.85 The corncrib with alley running through its sides usually has more storage capacity for ear corn. Sometimes the cribbing extends to the peak of the gable. Hamilton County, Iowa, 1981.

4.87 Corncrib made from railroad ties with square-notched corners. The modern "hewn" log crib? Projecting roof is characteristic of smokehouses and springhouses but also common on southern cribs. Rockcastle County, Kentucky.

4.86 Square crib built in 1910. Diagonal cribbing was often used because of the extra bracing it offered and for better shedding of water, especially in years before beveled cribbing was widely used. It is more time consuming to apply, however, and less efficient with material. Hamilton County, Iowa, 1983.

Decoration has never been a special feature of corncribs, certainly not to the extent it has on barns, though some farmers have added a flourish here and there. Bright red or pastel green paint in place of the usual white, barn red, or grey is a way of presenting one's best colors. The American flag is a natural for corncribs since its stripes match the horizontal cribbing. In contrast to the sublime and more attuned to our times perhaps is the graffiti crib, though here the farmer may not want to take full credit for its decoration.

Problems in Design and Engineering

In the most primitive cribs of rail or, nowadays, snow fence, the major problems are bursting from weight and pressure of the corn and spoilage due to lack of proper foundation or roof. Temporary cribs often give way to side pressures; unsupported snow fence was not meant to hold corn but often is expected to. Sometimes these cribs are set directly on the ground, which promotes rot and molding of the lowest foot or so of corn. Cribs supported by wood foundations sometimes collapse because of underestimated weight. Two-by-fours or -sixes are inadequate support for a 14-foot high crib.

4.88 Concrete crib on Steve West farm, Linn County, Iowa, 1982. Structure was formed and poured in 2-foot sections at a time. Ventilation holes were made by placing soaked corncobs in forms as concrete was poured, then punching them out when it set up.

4.89 As American as corn itself, the patriotic corncrib watches over a field of yellow tassels in August. Jones County, Iowa, 1983.

TWENTIETH CENTURY 77

4.90 Graffiti crib, perhaps not entirely the work of the farmer. Louisa County, Iowa, 1985.

4.92 This new crib gave way at the bottom with its first use due to inadequate joist support. Centre County, Pennsylvania, 1984.

Narrow single cribs are prone to blow over in strong winds, especially when empty. The top-heavy, V-shaped crib is jokingly said to be designed to do so, or would seem to be. Other cribs such as pole and wire, pole and snow fence, or steel mesh tend to collapse when empty if not braced properly or secured to a foundation.

The problems with modern corncribs are created by their size and the great quantities of corn they hold. The most serious problems result from settling and shifting of the corn as it dries and the side pressures created by this. Inside bracing tends to give way under the crushing load. Even small cribs will sag out of shape if their bracing is lost. Much of the weight of corn is exerted as side pressure against the walls, causing bulging and pushing off the cribbing.

4.91 Cribs of snow fence, two or three sections high, with board foundations or none are prone to burst under pressure of the corn. Tazewell County, Illinois, 1943.

4.93 Single crib tipped over by wind. Hamilton County, Iowa, 1981.

4.94 The walls of this old crib remain relatively straight, though there is evidence of bulging and sagging as shown by the wavy cribbing. Hamilton County, Iowa, 1983.

Another weight problem is with the overhead bins of double-crib/granary combinations. These are often not supported with adequate-sized floor joists or braced well enough for side pressures, especially to hold soybeans that are heavier even than corn and nearly twice the weight of oats. Older cribs, built for storage of oats in their bins, often have only 2 by 10 or 2 by 12 inch joists spaced 18 or 24 inches apart. In the 1950s and 1960s, as soybeans became a major crop of the Midwest in rotation with corn, stronger bin supports were essential. Rough three-by-twelves spaced on 12 inch centers were found adequate for the average 11 or 13 foot alley span. Side pressures, too, can cause bursting of deep bins and must be compensated for by installing tie rods across the bin near the bottom and middle. These are often evident from the gable end view of the corncrib.

Settling of the concrete foundation is caused by inadequate footings or soft underlying ground on a poorly selected site. It may also result from too skimpy a foundation. Concrete blocks, for example, are pushed unevenly into the ground under a crib's weight causing waves, bows, and bulges in the structure. Usually the massive foundations of larger cribs do not settle or break until very old, and then they may simply crumble away in harmony with the rest of the crib.

Mold is a problem with high and wide cribs where compaction is more severe and ventilation poor. Recommended crib widths depend upon the climate of a region, though 10-foot cribs are common in the heart of the Corn Belt where 8 feet might be better for drying. Corn picked clean dries better and compacts less than if lots of husks remain on the ears. It also should be dried to 20 to 25 percent moisture in the field before cribbing to prevent mold.

TWENTIETH CENTURY 79

4.95 Nails bend to keep a grip on the weathered cribbing as the corn pushes from behind. Adding more nails can't help for long as the rotted ends give way. Hamilton County, Iowa, 1983.

4.96 The bracing in this crooked crib has given out and it must be propped up. Columbia County, Wisconsin, 1982.

4.97 Weathered and rotting, this old crib foundation gradually settles, pulling the shelling door apart, but the whole structure keeps in step with its harmonious decay. Hamilton County, Iowa, 1983.

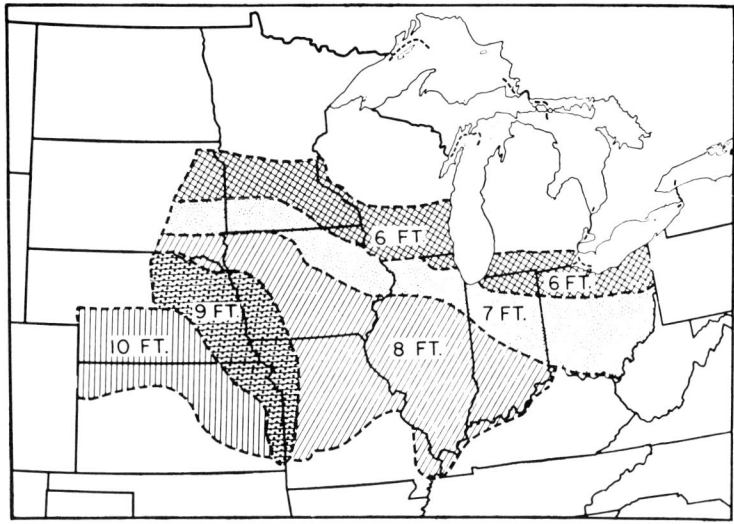

4.98 Crib widths recommended by the USDA but not strictly followed. Also suggested was orienting corncribs in a north-south direction so both sides would receive sunlight to help in drying, but this, too, was widely ignored.

When corn was picked by hand and scooped into the cribs, filling proceeded slowly enough for additional drying to occur during the process and for compaction to be minimized. Ears were generally picked cleaner, too, than with mechanical pickers. Settling was gradual so breakage of braces was less as well. The mechanical corn picker speeded up the process and with elevators making taller cribs possible, the corn was dumped more quickly and with greater shelling and compaction.

An early attempt to alleviate the problem of cribbing wet corn was the "corn drying rack," a trapdoor floor placed high in the crib between the rafters and inside studdings or at the plate line. This device was meant to hold the corn for a few days while it could dry somewhat more before dumping it into the crib. The contraption seems not to have been widely adopted, probably because it was inconvenient. Of course, filling by elevator was entirely too fast for use of such a device.

Problems with Insects

Insects have always been a problem in stored corn. One reason Indians parched or smoked some of their corn was to discourage insects. They also built their cribs upon high posts to keep out vermin such as ground-dwelling insects. Fires were set under the cribs of southern Indians — the smoke reduced weevil infestation. Southern farmers of today prefer corn with tight husks and they crib their corn unhusked to discourage the attack of weevils. An old method to keep out weevils was to add leaves of the China tree to each load of corn as it was cribbed. One of the earliest descriptions of an Indian corncrib, by John Lawson from North Carolina, mentions that it was built of saplings and plastered within and without with clay to seal out insects. A similar arrangement for an airtight crib to exclude weevils is described from Colorado County, Texas, in the U.S. Patent Office, *Agriculture Report for 1854*. Airtight pits, of course, were used by American Indians and the native peoples of many other lands to store food. Insects died in these from the carbon dioxide produced by their own respiration and that of the living grain.

In the Corn Belt insect damage is minimal or at least tolerable if corn is properly dried before cribbing and then stored only over winter. Long-term storage such as under the Ever-Normal Granary plan is an invitation to insect invasion. Corn "sealed" or "resealed" for two to five years under this program sometimes experienced heavy losses from insect damage. Insects not only destroy the grain directly, they invite molds to follow in their wake.

Problems with Rats

Protection from vermin has been a perennial problem with all grain storage and, in a way, the corncrib is an open invitation to invasion by all forms of life. Creatures such as squirrels and racoons relish the taste of corn and will enlarge the openings in cribbing enough for convenient feeding. Racoons will climb corncribbing as if it were a ladder in order to reach a select ear. They will also climb a crib ladder from the alley to reach the granary. More than one farmer has met a racoon in the narrow ladder space, much to the surprise of both. Of course, racoons are more fond of corn before it reaches the crib. They, like muskrats, love the taste of unripe corn and seem to enjoy sampling from many ears. Some birds, too, eat corn from cribs but house sparrows and pigeons are more destructive in making trashy nests and spreading their droppings. Pigeons will also break out a window of the cupola in making their escape from this seemingly natural trap.

Mice eat some corn and make nests of husks but rats do far more damage to both corn and crib. Rats destroy corn by gnawing on the ears and they undermine cribs or floors with their burrowing. They also chew through corncribbing, roofs, and bin walls to get at the grain. Each of the estimated 100 million rats in this country alone consumes or ruins $1 to $10 worth of food and feed per year, producing losses in excess of a billion dollars.

Rats have been unwelcome companions of humans for centuries. One of the least desirable accidental introductions to the New World, the brown rat not only destroys food and buildings, it spreads diseases such as typhus and dysentery to humans and cholera to hogs. Rats attack and kill poultry and will chew through the insulation on electric wires, causing fires.

Rats were stowaways on the first European ships to reach America and they quickly made themselves at home with stored corn just as they had in granaries of the Old Country. They took to American barns and came to use them as living quarters while the crib became their cafeteria.

The colonists first hid their corn (or tried to) by storing it in the attics above their kitchens. Later they carried on the traditions of both the Indians, who set their cribs upon poles as protection from squirrels, and the European farmers who built their granaries upon stones to help keep out rats. In both cases increased ventilation for drying was an equally important reason for such construction.

4.100 Sheet metal around base of crib for rat protection. Centre County, Pennsylvania, 1985.

4.99 Damage to cribbing by rats and probably raccoons in their successful efforts to reach the corn. White County, Indiana, 1982.

Prehistoric granaries dating from the Neolithic period of Europe are known to have had this rat protection. The foundation was made of four, six, or more sandstone blocks 2 to 3 feet high and tapered toward the top. Upon these were laid rounded capstones called "staddle stones," which were smoothened to keep rats from gaining a foothold and crawling over them. The granary floor joists of hewn timbers were laid upon these capstones and the remainder of the structure built of logs, stones, or brick.

In America the corncrib foundation was first made of poles skinned smooth, then of log sections or round stones, and later of barrels or concrete cylinders, perhaps cast in old pails. All these were attempts to keep the rat out. The capstone was replaced by the tin pie pan, proving, it would seem, that the corncrib is as American as apple pie. The pie pan when new and smooth was a deterrent to rats and its use was promoted until the late 1800s. As the metal rusted or was bent, however, the rats could gain a footing and crawl over at will.

Many strategies were devised to keep rats out though none was so common as the crib on posts with pie pan covers. Rats easily gnawed through boards so wire mesh was often used around the base of the crib. Of course the furry creatures merely crawled over this to make their entry holes. Sheet metal worked somewhat better but restricted ventilation. The modern steel-mesh corncrib is not ratproof either since the openings in the mesh are too large.

Doorways were often the weak link in rat protection, either because doors were left open or because they were not snug enough to prevent easy access. The notion of hinged, retractable steps leading to the doorway of an elevated crib might have been effective — but not if the farmer left the steps down. The so-called ratproof cribs made of perforated sheet steel, widely promoted between 1910 and 1940, were effective until the door became sprung and wouldn't close properly.

It was often recommended in early construction plans that a corncrib be set at least 18 inches aboveground to keep rats from jumping onto it. Two other reasons are usually given for the 18-inch space. One was so chickens could pick up shelled corn fallen through the bottom slats. The other was so "Fido" could get under the crib in search of rats.

Rats will burrow tunnels under a crib, especially the floor if it is made of wood. Their tunnels may so undermine a shallow foundation as to cause its settling and even topple the crib. By the end of the nineteenth century, however, larger corn cribs were being set on shorter, stouter foundations. For ventilation alone a smaller space was adequate. Very likely the higher crib was seen not to keep rats out anyway. Perhaps the most important consideration was that adding to the height of a crib made it harder to fill by hand scooping.

The one feature shared by all the attempts and devices to discourage rats was that they failed. The rat was indeed always king of the corncrib. A good rat dog might keep the population down a bit but not eliminate it.

4.101 The 11-foot alley is not wide enough even for today's moderate-sized equipment to fit inside. At least the front of this tractor is out of the rain. Note props supporting granary and end ties for cribs. Hamilton County, Iowa, 1983.

Not all dogs are equal when it comes to ratting. The real hunter is the rat terrier. This small dog can dig rats out of their burrows or intimidate them into surfacing. Instinctively the rat terrier knows at which entrance the rat will eventually show itself. Instantly the rat is caught by the head in the dog's jaws, pulled from its lair, and shaken furiously. The rat has no chance to bite or scratch. Its backbone is broken. Deliberately the excited dog will then crush the paralyzed rat's backbone from head to tail in its strong jaws and proudly display the corpse to its master.

The nonratter dog may assist in this work but is best advised to leave the actual catching to the rat terrier. Too often the rat is quicker than the dog and will get in a nasty nip before escaping.

Shelling out a corncrib may be a dirty job for humans but it makes a field day for rat dogs and cats. As the vermin lose their shelter of corn and husks they try to escape across open ground where the predators are waiting for them. Some farmers will assist in the hunt by placing a rotary mower near the crib and keep it running while they shell. Escaping rats and mice will seek shelter under the mower and get chopped.

In years past, an empty crib might cause the local rat population to move to one's neighbor only to return with the new harvest. This did not go unnoticed by the neighbor, incidentally, but since "rat-passing" was a mutual thing it worked out to no one's particular advantage, save the indefatigable touring rat.

It might seem that disease would have swept through the rat population occasionally as it did with rabbits or other wildlife but this didn't happen. Apparently rats throve on disease along with all the adversity man could throw their way.

The war on rats was fought on many fronts with many weapons, including guns, traps, dogs, poison, and gas. Carbon monoxide from car exhaust was supposed to be an effective rodent killer. In a USDA publication from 1938, *Corn Storage in the Ever-Normal Granary*, is shown a Model A Ford pumping exhaust into a corncrib. Some farmers tried the same thing with rat burrows. The rats didn't seem to pay proper attention. It was probably akin to pouring money down a rat hole.

Rat hunting was serious business. One farmer went shotgunning the damned rodents at night inside his storage shed. Carelessly, he aimed at a rat sitting just beyond the edge of a large round-bottomed kettle. At least some of the shot pellets fell short of their mark, followed the curved inside of the kettle and came back, hitting him in the face. Luckily he wasn't blinded. The rat escaped unharmed.

As a last resort, even exorcism has been called on to rid one's property of rats. At least so folklore has it from the nineteenth century. Apparently a farmer whose crops were short one year wrote a letter to the rats explaining his plight — that he could not afford to keep them through the winter, that he had been very kind to them, and that for their own good they should leave him and go to his neighbors who had more grain. He pinned this plea to a post in his barn for the rats to read. It probably worked, too, if he was really being honest with the rats about having little or no grain. They won't hang around for scarcity.

It took science to get even with the rat, or at least catch up a bit. About 1950 it was recognized that the drugs known as coumarins, which prevent blood from clotting, might be used to kill rodents. Scientists working under a grant from the Wisconsin Alumni Research Foundation (WARF) produced a new rodenticide appropriately named Warfarin.

Now there had been rat poisons before but they mostly didn't work. Rats wouldn't cooperate and eat them or if they did, they refused to die. Sneak feeding them something that made them bleed to death internally was pretty "ratty" of humans. Warfarin and soon other commercial products did that. In the annals of ratdom this was an ominous day, hardly fair play. At last humans had a fighting chance against this age-old enemy. The cause for celebration was tempered, however, as resistant strains soon began to appear. Rats, like many pests, are real evolutionists. They practice survival of the fittest; and what is fit for them is a real test for humans.

4.102 The grain dryer here fits inside the alley of this unused crib but the gable had to be cut first. Hamilton County, Iowa, 1983.

84 TWENTIETH CENTURY

Alternative Uses

Although the corncrib was originally built for the singular purpose of storing ear corn and later in overhead bins for shelled grain, it has found some versatility for other uses. In earlier days after the cribs were emptied in the spring they might be used by the brooding or "setting" hens to hatch out their chicks. The alley of many an existing double corncrib today continues to be used for machinery storage, though modern implements and tractors are often too large to completely fit inside.

Even if abandoned for corn storage, cribs may be used to house bags of fertilizer, cans of herbicide, or assorted junk. They are also used for drying and storing firewood, garden produce, or bales of straw and hay. More often, however, cribs stand empty unless they have been converted to storage of shelled corn or soybeans by covering or replacing the cribbing with tight-fitted siding or boarding up the inside. Flexible liners are available for grain storage in wire cribs.

4.104 This little crib shed is used for storing many things, but they have little to do with corn. Mille Lacs County, Minnesota, 1983.

4.103 Here the corncrib alley has become a cattle shed; the cribs are used to store hay. Isanti County, Minnesota, 1983.

4.105 Storing firewood. Sauk County, Wisconsin, 1982.

4.106 Straw storage in a keystone crib. Isanti County, Minnesota, 1983.

4.107–108 Corncribs are sometimes converted to shelled corn storage and become part of complete grain-handling systems. Wright County, Iowa, 1983.

Corncribs have generally always stood empty for part of the year, of course, so casual observations can be deceiving, especially from spring through summer. The truly abandoned crib is commonly found in marginal corn-producing areas where many farmers have quit growing the crop or in the heart of corn country where technology has bypassed crib storage of ear corn.

Corncribs have not received the attention that barns have in preservation or remodeling. Perhaps they aren't as picturesque, though some do rival barns in design. There is less nostalgia associated with cribs and they may be less adaptable to recycling, partly because the usable open space is less than in barns. Remodeling has gained some popularity in recent years, however, as a means of saving money in response to rising costs of materials and labor. By saving the roof and structural frame while residing the exterior and gutting the interior, a machine shed can be had for about half the cost of a new building.

Perhaps one of the most unusual new uses for an old corncrib is to convert it to a house. Some carpenters in the Midwest have made a specialty of such conversions from barns and corncribs. An example from Illinois is illustrated in the August 1979 issue of *House and Garden.* One problem in such a conversion is how to find living space among the heavy framing, bracing, and timbers. In the Illinois example the alley became a living room, overhead bins, loft bedrooms. Cost of this remodeling was $25,000, probably ten times that of the original building (even in terms of comparable dollars) but reasonable for a house.

Corncribs have an earlier history of conversion to living quarters, especially log cribs. A hero of World War I, Sgt. Alvin York, was born in a cabin made from a corncrib.

If old cribs have found new uses, the reverse is also true. Buildings such as small houses and one-room country schoolhouses have been converted to corn storage. Old railroad cars, especially stock cars, would seem to be made-to-order corncribs. Most are used as storage sheds, granaries, or livestock shelters, however.

4.109 Outside the Corn Belt such empty cribs may only look abandoned but as often as not are filled at every harvest, then shelled out by summer. Long single cribs such as these were commonly built in areas where separate granaries were available and it never became a custom to build corncribs with overhead bins. Huntingdon County, Pennsylvania, 1981.

4.110 Apparently abandoned, this pole, wire, and wood-slat crib has been outdated by newer technologies of harvest and storage. Hamilton County, Iowa, 1981.

4.111 A corncrib converted to machine shed by gutting the interior, adding new siding and oversized sliding doors. Watonwan County, Minnesota, 1983.

4.112 A small house used as a corncrib. Most of the siding has been replaced with rough cribbing, there is some snow-fence lining, windows are boarded up, and a shelling door has been cut. An old oil burner lies in front. Hamilton County, Iowa, 1982.

Decay and Falling to Ruin

Almost overnight the corncrib became outdated by the new harvest technologies, artificial drying, and storage facilities adopted by most large-scale corn farmers in the 1960s. New early maturing hybrid corns adapted to combine harvesting also contributed to the changeover. Many cribs would never see another ear of corn. Not all farmers gave up their corn pickers but more corncribs are now permanently empty than are ever filled.

In areas of corn production primarily for on-farm use, however, the corncrib still fulfills its original function. Numerous photographs in this book confirm that the corncrib is not yet an anachronism. Even in the Corn Belt itself, record crop years of the mid-1980s, combined with a shortage of storage facilities, have called some abandoned corncribs back into service.

4.113 A grain-drying and storage system dwarfs the crib and leaves it at the sidelines. Cedar County, Iowa, 1983.

4.114 This old crib now serves mainly as a support for the auger conveyers leading from bin to bin. Hamilton County, Iowa, 1983.

The corncrib is still used for ear corn on farms that feed livestock.

4.115 Dodge County, Wisconsin, 1983.

Many old corncribs do sit waiting for the bulldozer or torch, of course. Where buildings are taxed as "improvements" regardless of condition, there is an incentive to take them down if unused. A farmer in central Ohio commented that the old steel-strap crib I'd stopped to photograph was costing him about $30 per year in taxes. Perhaps he hadn't thought about the old crib for years but this self-reminder was enough — the next year it was gone.

4.117   In Amish country the corncrib is more than a picture in a book.

4.116   Lancaster County, Pennsylvania, 1985.

Corncribs in various stages of ruin.

4.118   Crib shed attached to collapsed barn being scavenged for lumber. Centre County, Pennsylvania, 1983.

Entire farmsteads, when unused, are even larger tax burdens and have been leveled by burning and bulldozing at increasing rates in recent years as Midwest farms have grown in size. A primary goal of removing corncribs from fields or even leveling whole sets of farm buildings is to eliminate obstacles to farming, especially important for using large equipment.

4.119 Falling apart as it was built, board by board. White County, Indiana, 1982.

4.120 This old steel-strap crib hadn't stored corn for several years so it was taken down to save taxes. Hancock County, Ohio, 1981.

4.121 A farmstead no longer a home, the first stage toward elimination, though the barn and crib here are still in use. Often the flat land is more valuable and certainly easier to work if free of obstructions. Wright County, Iowa, 1983.

Corncribs one step from removal due to road and urban development.

4.123 A corncrib-carriage shed, part of a historic farmstead, known locally as the Hoffer Farm or Nissely Farm, near Middletown, Pennsylvania. John Motter was the nineteenth-century owner responsible for building several structures in an architectural style known as Carpenter Gothic. Dauphin County, Pennsylvania, 1982.

4.122 This pile of earth and rubble is all that remains of a farmstead. Most likely a bulldozer will bury the concrete foundations and level the ground so it can be farmed over. Keokuk County, Iowa, 1983.

4.124 Shopping malls love to grow big parking lots on flat and productive agricultural land. Columbia County, Wisconsin, 1982.

Encroaching urban development is another major reason for removing farm buildings. Real estate and road developments threaten farmland and buildings by placing a value on rural property much higher than that returned by the commodities produced from the land.

4.125   This corncrib is trapped between a four-lane highway and two motels. There is no escape. LaSalle County, Illinois, 1983.

TWENTIETH CENTURY

Tearing down the corncrib.

4.126 A relatively recent crib with overhead granary, valuable for its lumber and the space it occupies in this field. Hamilton County, Iowa, 1983.

4.127 An older crib, sold for $150 in salvage. The hand-operated gas pump is likely worth more than that as an antique. Hamilton County, Iowa, 1983.

It is not easy to dismantle a corncrib in order to salvage the lumber, yet some cribs are being taken down this way because of the cost of new lumber. Cribs are heavily laced with nails, clinched where possible, so it is not a pleasure to work at undoing them. More often a few boards are scavenged from a crib as needed and the structure is gradually skeletonized.

Many old corncribs are left to decay in their own good time. The large ones are like majestic old castles, drafty and cavernous, moaning gently in the wind.

4.128 This corncrib appears to be coming down gradually as lumber is needed elsewhere. Washington County, Iowa, 1983.

4.129 Battered by weather and years of corn but standing tall, patiently waiting for time. Hamilton County, Iowa, 1983.

4.130   Like a majestic old castle, moaning gently in the wind.
Hamilton County, Iowa, 1982.

Bibliography

INDIAN CORN AND STORAGE

Lynn Marie Alex. *Oneota*. Office of the State Archeologist Educational Series 6. Iowa City: Univ. of Iowa, 1976.

Edgar Anderson. *Corn Before Columbus*. Des Moines: Pioneer Hi-Bred Corn Company, n.d.

William Bartram. *Travels through North and South Carolina, Georgia, East and West Florida, The Cherokee Country...* 1791. Reprint. Edited by Francis Harper. New Haven: Yale Univ. Press, 1958.

M. K. Bennett. "The Food Economy of the New England Indians, 1605–75." *Journal of Political Economy* 63(1955):369–97.

Lucien Carr. "The Mounds of the Mississippi Valley, Historically Considered." *Smithsonian Institution Annual Report 1891*(1893):503–99.

Jacques Cartier. *The Voyages of Jacques Cartier*. Translated by H. P. Biggar. Publications of the Public Archives of Canada, 11. Ottawa: F. A. Acland, 1924.

Edward F. Castetter and Willis H. Bell. *Pima and Papago Indian Agriculture*. Albuquerque: Univ. of New Mexico Press, 1942.

———. *Yuman Indian Agriculture*. Albuquerque: Univ. of New Mexico Press, 1951.

G. N. Collins. "Notes on Agricultural History of Maize." *Agricultural History Society Papers* 2(1919):411–29.

Harold E. Driver and William C. Massey. *Comparative Studies of North American Indians*. Transactions, American Philosophical Society, n.s., 47, pt. 2. Philadelphia, 1957, 165–456.

A Gentleman of Elvas: Narratives of the Career of Hernando de Soto. 2 vols. Translated by Buckingham Smith. New York: Allerton, 1922, vol. 1.

Handbook of North American Indians. Vol. 15. *Northeast*. Edited by Bruce G. Trigger. Washington: Smithsonian Institution Press, 1978.

Conrad E. Heidenreich. *Huronia: A History and Geography of the Huron Indians 1600–50*. Toronto: McClelland and Stewart, 1971.

Efraim Hernández Xolocotzi. "Maize Granaries in Mexico." *Botanical Museum Leaflets*, Harvard University 13(1949):153–92 + plates.

W. W. Hill. *The Agricultural and Hunting Methods of the Navaho Indians*. New Haven: Yale University Publications in Anthropology 18, 1938.

Henry Hudson. "Description of New Netherlands." In *Extracts from the New World or a Description of the West Indies*, edited by John de Laet. New York Historical Society Collections, 2d. ser. 1(1841):281–316.

Hugh Iltis. "From Teosinte to Maize: The Catastrophic Sexual Transmutation." *Science* 222(1983):886–94.

Stephen C. Jett and Virginia E. Spencer. *Navajo Architecture, Forms, History, Distributions*. Tucson: Univ. of Arizona Press, 1981.

Clyde Kluckhohn, W. W. Hill, and Lucy Wales Kluckhohn. *Navaho Material Culture*. Cambridge: Harvard Univ. Press, 1971.

Father Lafitau. *Customs of the American Indians Compared with the Customs of the First Times*. Vol. 2. Edited and translated by W. N. Fenton and E. L. Moore. Publications of the Champlain Society 48–49. Toronto: Champlain Society, 1977.

John Lawson. *Lawson's History of North Carolina*. 1714. Reprint. Edited by Frances Latham Harriss. Richmond: Garrett and Massie, 1952.

Robert H. Lowie. *Indians of the Plains*. New York: Natural History Press, 1963.

Paul C. Mangelsdorf. "The Origin of Corn." *Scientific American* 255 (1986): 80–86.

Maya Subsistence. Edited by Kent V. Flannery. New York: Academic Press, 1982.

Lewis H. Morgan. *Houses and House-Life of the American Aborigines*. Vol. 4. Contributions to North American Ethnology, 1881. Chicago: Univ. of Chicago Press, 1965.

Arthur C. Parker. *Iroquois Uses of Maize and Other Food Plants*. New York State Museum, Museum Bulletin 144, 1910.

Frederic B. Perkins, translator. *Narrative of Le Moyne, an Artist Who Accompanied the French Expedition to Florida under Laudonniere, 1564*. Boston: Osgood, 1875.

Jerome C. Rose, Barbara A. Burnett, and Mark W. Blaeuer. "Paleopathology and the Origins of Maize Agriculture in the Lower Mississippi Valley and Caddoan Culture Areas." In *Paleopathology at the Origins of Agriculture*, edited by Mark Nathan Cohen and George J. Armelayos, 393–424. Orlando: Academic Press, 1984.

Neal Salisbury. *Manitou and Providence, Indians and Europeans, and the Making of New England, 1500–1643*. New York: Oxford Univ. Press, 1982.

Francois Sigaut. "Significance of Underground Storage in Traditional Systems of Grain Production." In *Controlled Atmosphere Storage of Grains*, edited by J. Shejbal, 3–38. New York: Elsevier, 1980.

Charles W. Spellman. "The Agriculture of the Early North Florida Indians." *Florida Anthropologist* 1(1948):37–48.

Henry M. Steece. "Corn Culture among the Indians of the Southwest." *Natural History* 21(1921):414–24.

K. M. Stewart. "Mojave Indian Agriculture." *Masterkey* 40(1966):5–15.

Bonnie W. Styles. "Early Native Americans in Illinois." *Living Museum* 46, no. 2(1984):19–31.

John R. Swanton. *Indians of the Southwestern United States*. Bulletin, Bureau of American Ethnology 137, 1946. Grosse Point, Mich.: Scholarly Press, 1969.

H. Garrison Wilkes. "Mexico and Central America as a Centre for the Origin of Agriculture and the Evolution of Maize." *Crop Improvement* 6, no. 1(1979):1–18.

George F. Will and George E. Hyde. *Corn among the Indians of the Upper Missouri*. 1917. Reprint. Lincoln: Univ. of Nebraska Press, 1964.

COLONIAL PERIOD

Wayne Andrews. *Architecture, Ambition, and Americans: A Social History of American Architecture.* Rev. ed. New York: Free Press, 1978.

Stanley Baron. *Brewed in America: A History of Beer and Ale in the United States.* Boston: Little, Brown, 1962.

Douglas E. Bowers. "American Agriculture: The Contributions of German-Americans." In *Symposium on German-American Agriculture and Folk Culture*, edited by Alan E. Fusonie and Donna Jean Fusonie. *Journal NAL Associates*, n.s., 9, no. 1–4(1984):1–12.

Martin S. Briggs. *The Homes of the Pilgrim Fathers in England and America, 1620–1685.* New York: Oxford Univ. Press, 1932.

John R. Brodhead. *Documents Relative to the Colonial History of the State of New York.* Edited by E. B. O'Callaghan. 15 vols. Albany: Weed, Parsons, 1856, vol. 1.

Philip A. Bruce. *Economic History of Virginia in the Seventeenth Century.* New York: Macmillan, 1896.

Thomas Budd. *Good Order Established in Pennsylvania and New Jersey.* 1685. Reprint with introduction and notes by Frederick J. Shepard. Cleveland: Burrows Brothers, 1902.

Eva L. Butler. "Algonkian Culture and Use of Maize." *Bulletin Archeological Society Connecticut* 22(1948):3–39.

Lyman Carrier. *The Beginnings of Agriculture in America.* New York: McGraw-Hill, 1923.

G. N. Collins. "Notes on the Agricultural History of Maize." *Agricultural History Society Papers* 2(1919):411–29.

Everett E. Edwards. "American Agriculture: The First 300 Years," 171–276. In *Farmers in a Changing World: USDA Yearbook of Agriculture 1940.*

Robert F. Ensminger. "A Search for the Origin of the Pennsylvania Barn." *Pennsylvania Folklife* 30, no. 2(1980):50–71.

Sigurd Erixon. "West European Connections and Cultural Relations." *Folk-Liv* 2(1938):137–72.

Paul W. Gates. "Problems of Agricultural History 1790–1840." In *Farming in the New Nation: Interpreting American Agriculture 1790–1840*, edited by Darwin P. Kelsey, 33–58. Washington: Agricultural History Society, 1972.

Dorothy Giles. *Singing Valleys: The Story of Corn.* New York: Random House, 1940.

Henry Glassie. "The Barns of Appalachia." *Mountain Life and Work* 41, no. 2(1965):21–30.

Joseph Jackson. *American Colonial Architecture.* Philadelphia: David McKay, 1924.

Diamond Jenness. *The Indians of Canada.* 7th ed. (Bulletin 65, Anthropological Series 15, 1932. National Museum of Canada). Toronto: Univ. of Toronto Press, 1977.

Amandus Johnson. *The Swedish Settlements on the Delaware...1638–1664.* 2 vols. Philadelphia: Univ. of Pennsylvania Press, 1911. Vol. 1.

Terry G. Jordan. *American Log Buildings: An Old World Heritage.* Chapel Hill: Univ. of North Carolina Press, 1985.

Peter Kalm. "Peter Kalm's Description of Maize, How It Is Planted and Cultivated in North America, Together with the Many Uses of This Crop Plant." Translated by Ester L. Larsen. *Agricultural History* 9(1935):98–117.

Gloria L. Main. *Tobacco Colony: Life in Early Maryland, 1650–1720.* Princeton: Princeton Univ. Press, 1982.

Edmund S. Morgan. *American Slavery, American Freedom, the Ordeal of Colonial Virginia.* New York: Norton, 1975.

Narratives of Early Pennsylvania, West New Jersey and Delaware, 1630–1707, edited by Albert C. Myers. New York: Scribners, 1912.

New Haven Colony Historical Society, *Ancient Town Records.* 2 vols. Edited by Franklin B. Dexter. New Haven: Printed for the Society, 1917, vol. 1, 1649–1662.

Charles H. Pope. *The Plymouth Scrap Book.* Boston: C. E. Goodspeed, 1918.

Public Records of the Colony of Connecticut 1665. Wills and Inventories. Transcribed by J. Hammond Trumbull. Hartford: Brown and Parsons, 1850.

Allen Walker Read. "The Comment of British Travelers on Early American Terms Relating to Agriculture." *Agricultural History* 7(1933):99–109.

Darrett B. Rutman. *Husbandmen of Plymouth: Farms and Villages in the Old Colony, 1620–1692.* Boston: Beacon Press, 1967.

Neal Salisbury. "Squanto: Last of the Patuxets." In *Struggle and Survival in Colonial America*, edited by D. G. Sweet and G. B. Nash, 228–46. Berkeley: Univ. of California Press, 1981.

George E. K. Smith. *Sweden Builds.* Stockholm: A. Bonnier, 1950.

James W. Thompson. *A History of Livestock Raising in the United States, 1607–1860.* Agricultural History Series 5. Washington: USDA, 1942.

Leon de Valinger, Jr. "The Burning of the Whorekill, 1673." *Pennsylvania Magazine* 74(1950):473–89.

Robert R. Walcott. "Husbandry in Colonial New England." *New England Quarterly* 9(1936):218–52.

Edward Ward. "A Trip to New England, 1699." In *Five Travel Scripts, Commonly Attributed to Edward Ward.* New York: Columbia Univ. Press, 1933.

C. A. Weslanger. "Log Structures in New Sweden during the Seventeenth Century." *Delaware History* 5(1952):77–95.

———. *Dutch Explorers, Traders and Settlers in the Delaware Valley 1609–1664.* Philadelphia: Univ. of Pennsylvania Press, 1961.

———. *The English on the Delaware: 1610–1682.* New Brunswick: Rutgers Univ. Press, 1967.

PIONEER SPIRIT AND WESTWARD EXPANSION

R. L. Ardrey. *American Agricultural Implements.* 1894. Reprint. New York: Arno Press, 1972.

Theodore C. Blegen. *Land of Their Choice.* St. Paul: Univ. of Minnesota Press, 1955.

Allan G. Bogue. *From Prairie to Corn Belt: Farming on the Illinois and Iowa Prairies in the Nineteenth Century.* Chicago: Univ. of Chicago Press, 1963.

James C. Bonner. *A History of Georgia Agriculture 1732–1860.* Athens: Univ. of Georgia Press, 1964.

Marilyn S. Brinkman and William T. Morgan. *Light from the Hearth: Central Minnesota Pioneers and Early Architecture.* St. Cloud: North Star Press, 1982.

Brian Coffey. "From Shanty to House: Log Construction in Nineteenth Century Ontario." *Material Culture* 16(1984):61–75.

Clarence Danhof. "Farm-making Costs and the 'Safety Valve': 1850–60." *Journal of Political Economy* 49(1941):317–59.

———. *Change in Agriculture: The Northern United States, 1820–1870.* Cambridge: Harvard Univ. Press, 1969.

Victor C. Dieffenbach. "The Corn-crib." *Pennsylvania Dutchman* 5, no. 9(1954):11–12.

Everett E. Edwards. "American Agriculture: The First 300 Years." 171–276. In *Farmers in a Changing World: USDA Yearbook of Agriculture 1940.*

Gilbert Fite. *The Farmer's Frontier 1865–1900.* New York: Holt, Rinehart and Winston, 1966.

Paul W. Gates. *The Farmer's Age: Agriculture 1815–1860.* Vol. 3 of *The Economic History of the United States.* New York: Holt, Rinehart and Winston, 1951.

Henry Glassie. "The Smaller Outbuildings of the Southern Mountains." *Mountain Life and Work* 40, no. 1(1964):21–25.

———. The Old Barns of Appalachia. *Mountain Life and Work* 4, no. 2(1965):21–30.

John Fraser Hart. *The Look of the Land.* Englewood Cliffs: Prentice-Hall, 1975.

George B. Hartman. "The Iowa Sawmill Industry." *Iowa Journal of History and Politics* 40(1942):52–93.

Donald A. Hutslar. "The Ohio Farmstead: Farm Buildings as Cultural Artifacts." *Ohio History* 90(1981):221–37.

W. A. Lloyd, J. I. Falconer, and C. E. Thorne. *The Agriculture of Ohio.* Ohio Agriculture Experiment Station Bulletin 326, 1918.

Amos Long, Jr. "Pennsylvania Corncribs." *Pennsylvania Folklife* 14, no. 1(1964):16–23.

———. *Farmsteads and Their Buildings.* Lebanon, Pa.: Applied Art Publishers, 1972.

———. *The Pennsylvania German Family Farm.* Publications of the Pennsylvania German Society vol. 4. Breinigsville, Pa.: Pennsylvania German Society, 1972.

Sally McMurray. "Progressive Farm Families and Their Houses, 1830–1855: A Study in Independent Design." *Agricultural History* 58(1984):330–46.

Howard W. Marshall. *Folk Architecture in Little Dixie.* Columbia: Univ. of Missouri Press, 1981.

William L. Montell and Michael L. Morse. *Kentucky Folk Architecture.* Lexington: Univ. Press of Kentucky, 1976.

Allen G. Noble. *Wood, Brick, and Stone: The North American Settlement Landscape.* Vol. 2, *Barns and Farm Structures.* Amherst: Univ. of Massachusetts Press, 1984.

William Radford. *Radford's Combined House and Barn Plan Book.* Chicago: Radford Architectural Co., 1908.

Leo Rogin. *The Introduction of Farm Machinery in Its Relation to the Productivity of Labor in the United States During the Nineteenth Century.* University of California Publications in Economics vol. 9. Berkeley: Univ. of California Press, 1931.

Fred A. Shannon. *The Farmer's Last Frontier: Agriculture, 1860–1897.* Vol. 5 of *Economic History of the United States.* New York: Farrar and Rinehart, 1945.

Eric Sloane. *An Age of Barns.* New York: Balantine Books, 1974.

Gustav E. M. Unonius. *A Pioneer in Northwest America 1841–1858: The Memoirs of Gustav Unonius.* 2 vols. Translated by Jonas O. Backlund and edited by Nils W. Olsson. Minneapolis: Univ. of Minnesota Press, 1950–60.

TWENTIETH CENTURY: ERA OF GROWTH

J. Richard Adams. "Trends in Fertilizers," 194–200. In *Soil: USDA Yearbook of Agriculture,* 1957.

Agricultural Statistics 1965. Washington: USDA, 1965.

Wallace Ashby. "Fifty Years of Development in Farm Buildings." *Agricultural Engineering* 38(1957):426–32, 459.

M. B. Bogue. "The Swamp Land Act and Wet Land Utilization in Illinois, 1850–1890." *Agricultural History* 25(1951):169–80.

Albert P. Brodell and Harold R. Walker. *Harvesting Corn for Grain.* USDA Statistical Bulletin 129, 1953.

E. C. Brooks. *The Story of Corn in the Westward Migration.* Chicago: Rand McNally, 1916.

William L. Brown. "Wallace and the Development of Hybrid Corn." Paper presented at the Henry A. Wallace and Iowa Agriculture Conference June 4, 1983, Des Moines, Iowa.

Ovid M. Butler. *The Distribution of Softwood Lumber in the Middle West: Retail Distribution.* Studies of the Lumber Industry pt. 9. USDA Report no. 116, 1918.

Victor S. Clark. *History of Manufactures in the United States, 1893–1928.* Vol. 3. New York: Peter Smith, 1949.

Corn Storage in the Ever Normal Granary. U.S. Agricultural Adjustment Administration, 38-Corn-2, 1938.

A. Richard Crabb. *The Hybrid-Corn Makers: Prophets of Plenty.* New Brunswick: Rutgers Univ. Press, 1947.

A. Kirk Crawford. "Structural Analysis and Design of a Corn Crib." Masters thesis, Iowa State College, 1939.

David B. Danbom. *The Resisted Revolution: Urban America and the Industrialization of Agriculture, 1900–1930.* Ames: Iowa State Univ. Press, 1979.

J. B. Davidson. *Agricultural Machinery.* New York: Wiley, 1931.

Doane Ideas on Farm Buildings. St. Louis: Doane Agricultural Service, 1951.

Hiram M. Drache. *Beyond the Furrow: Some Keys to Successful Farming in the Twentieth Century.* Danville: Interstate, 1976.

———. "Midwest Agriculture: Changing with Technology." In *Two Centuries of American Agriculture,* edited by Vivian Wiser, 290–302. Washington: Agricultural History Society, 1976.

———. *Plowshares to Printouts.* Danville: Interstate, 1985.

Ed Edwin. *Feast or Famine.* New York: Charterhouse, 1974.

William D. Emerson. *History and Incidents of Indian Corn and its Culture.* Cincinnati: Wrightson, 1878.

James M. Fitch. "Uses of the Artistic Past." In *American Folklife,* edited by Don Yoder, 27–49. Austin: Univ. of Texas Press, 1976.

D. A. FitzGerald. *Corn and Hogs Under the Agricultural Adjustment Act.* Brookings Institute Pamphlet Series 12. Washington: Brookings Institute, 1934.

James G. Frazer. *The New Golden Bough.* Edited by Theodor H. Gaster. New York: Criterion Books, 1959.

Robert F. Fries. *Empire in Pine.* Madison: State Historical Society of Wisconsin, 1951.

Henry Giese. "Design Problems for Combined Crib and Granary." *Agricultural Engineering* 21(1940):283–85.

———. "Trends in Farm Structures." In *A Century of Farming in Iowa 1846–1946,* 250–61. Ames: Iowa State College Press, 1946.

Dorothy Giles. *Singing Valleys: The Story of Corn.* New York: Random House, 1940.

Grain Elevators of North America. 5th ed. Chicago: Grain and Feeds Journals, 1942.

Roy B. Gray and E. M. Dieffenbach. "Fifty Years of Tractor Development in the U.S.A." *Agricultural Engineering* 38(1957):388–97.

B. D. Halstead. *Barn Plans and Outbuildings.* New York: Orange Judd, 1890.

Nicholas P. Hardeman. *Shucks, Shocks, and Hominy*

Blocks. Baton Rouge: Louisiana State Univ. Press, 1981.

Nigel Harvey. *Industrial Archaeology of Farming in England and Wales.* London: B. T. Batsford, 1980.

Robert Hendrickson. *More Cunning than Man: A Social History of Rats and Men.* New York: Stein and Day, 1983.

Ralph W. Hidy, Frank E. Hill, and Allan Nevins. *Timber and Men: The Weyerhaeuser Story.* New York: Macmillan, 1963.

W. M. Hurst and L. M. Church. *Power and Machinery in Agriculture.* USDA Miscellaneous Publication 157, 1933.

I and T Catalog File, 1950 Edition. Kansas City: Implement and Tractor, 1949.

K. D. Jacob. "Materials and Mixtures," 200–210. In *Soil: USDA Yearbook of Agriculture,* 1957.

Paul C. Johnson. *Farm Power in the Making of America.* Des Moines: Wallace-Homestead, 1978.

Sherman E. Johnson. *Changes in American Farming.* USDA Miscellaneous Publication 707, 1949.

William H. Johnson and Benson J. Lamp. *Principles, Equipment and Systems for Corn Harvesting.* Wooster, Ohio: Agricultural Consulting Associates, 1966.

W. H. Jordan. "Fertilizers: Their Kinds and Characteristics." In *Cyclopedia of American Agriculture.* 4 vols. Edited by L. H. Bailey, 1:458–71. New York: Macmillan, 1907.

E. J. Kahn, Jr. "The Staffs of Life: I. The Golden Thread." *New Yorker,* 18 June 1984, 46–88.

M. A. R. Kelley. *Corncribs for the Corn Belt.* USDA Farmer's Bulletin 1701, 1933.

Wayne E. Kiefer "An Agricultural Settlement Complex in Indiana." *Annals Association American Geographers* 62(1972):487–506.

Mack N. Leath, Lynn H. Meyer, and Lowell D. Hill. *U.S. Corn Industry.* USDA Agriculture Economic Report 479, 1982.

Oscar H. Lowery. "Utilization of Lumber in Grain Storage Structures." Masters thesis, Iowa State College, 1941.

H. F. McColly. "Fifty Years of Farm Machinery." *Agricultural Engineering* 38(1957):398–404.

Alan I Marcus. *Agricultural Science and the Quest for Legitimacy.* Ames: Iowa State Univ. Press, 1985.

Peter C. Marzio. "Carpentry in the Southern Colonies during the Eighteenth Century with Emphasis on Maryland and Virginia." *Winterthur Portfolio* 7(1972):229–50.

Albert S. Mowery. "The Construction, Age, and Condition of Farm Buildings in the United States and the Implications of These Factors for the Farm Mechanics Phase of Instruction in Vocational Agriculture." Ph.D. diss., Pennsylvania State University, 1957.

"New Corn Husking Record." *Wallaces' Farmer* 57(1932):621, 630.

Allen G. Noble. "The Corn Crib: Evolution of an American Farm Structure." Paper presented at the Pioneer America Society meeting, Macomb, Illinois, 7 October 1983.

———. *Wood, Brick, and Stone: The North American Settlement Landscape.* Vol. 2 of *Barns and Farm Structures.* Amherst: Univ. of Massachusetts Press, 1984.

William N. Parker. "A Note on Regional Culture in the Corn Harvest." In *Farming in the New Nation,* edited by Darwin P. Kelsey, 181–89. Washington: Agricultural History Society, 1972.

Graeme R. Quick and Wesley F. Buchele. *The Grain Harvesters.* St. Joseph, Mich.: American Society of Agricultural Engineers, 1978.

Wayne D. Rasmussen, Gladys L. Baker, and James S. Ward. *A Short History of Agricultural Adjustment, 1933–75.* USDA Agriculture Information Bulletin 391, 1976.

Joe B. Richardson. "The Structural Requirements of Grain Storage Buildings." Masters thesis, Iowa State College, 1938.

Howard G. Roepke. "Changes in Corn Production in the Northern Margin of the Corn Belt." *Agricultural History* 33(1959):126–32.

Bryce Ryan. "A Study in Technological Diffusion." *Rural Sociology* 13(1948):273–85.

Devendra Sahal. *Patterns of Technological Innovation.* Reading, Mass.: Addison-Wesley, 1981.

James R. Schimmer and Allen G. Noble. "The Evolution of the Corn Crib with Special Reference to Putnam County, Illinois." *Pioneer America Society Transactions* 7(1984):21–33.

John T. Schlebecker. *Whereby We Thrive: A History of American Farming, 1607–1972.* Ames: Iowa State Univ. Press, 1975.

George H. Seferovich. "Symbols of Modern Mechanization." *Implement and Tractor* 76, no. 4(1961):30–31.

L. W. Smith and L. W. Wood. *History of Yard Lumber Size Standards.* Madison: U.S. Forest Products Laboratory, 1964.

Marvanna S. Smith. *Chronological Landmarks in American Agriculture.* USDA Agriculture Information Bulletin 425, 1979.

Norman C. Teter and Henry Giese. "New Barns for Old," 218–30. In *Power to Produce: USDA Yearbook of Agriculture,* 1960.

Henry A. Wallace. "Corn and the Midwestern Farmer." *Proceedings American Philosophical Society* 100(1956):455–66.

Henry A. Wallace and William C. Brown. *Corn and its Early Fathers.* East Lansing: Michigan State Univ. Press, 1956.

C. H. Wendel. *Encyclopedia of American Farm Tractors.* Sarasota: Crestline Publishing, 1979.

Ralph Whitlock. *The English Farm.* London: J. M. Dent, 1983.

Reynold M. Wik. "Henry Ford's Tractors and American Agriculture." *Agricultural History* 38(1964):79–86.

Michael Williams. *Great Tractors.* Poole, Dorset: Blanford Press, 1982.

———. *Classic Farm Tractors.* Poole, Dorset: Blanford Press, 1984.

C. J. Zintheo. *Corn Harvesting Machinery.* U.S. Office of Experiment Stations Bulletin 173, 1907.

Photographic Credits

Photos by author unless otherwise attributed

1.1 From Hernández Xolocotzi 1949.
1.2 Photo by Milton S. Snow.
1.3 National Archives.
1.4 (1962), 1.5 (1964), 1.12 (1978). Photos by Garrison Wilkes.
1.6 From Lowie 1963.
1.8 From Morgan.
1.9 Drawing by James E. Price.
1.10 From Lorant 1965.
1.11 From Parker 1910.
2.1 From Smith 1950.
2.2 Abby Aldrich Rockefeller Folk Art Center, Williamsburg, Virginia.
2.3 Lincoln Boyhood National Memorial, Lincoln City, Indiana.
2.4 Photo by Moorehouse, National Archives.
2.5 Photo by Thomas L. Williams, courtesy of National Historical Park.
2.6 *American Agriculturalist*, February 1877.
2.8 National Museum of Finland.
2.10 National Gallery of Art.
2.12, 3.19 State Historical Society of Wisconsin.
2.13, 2.14, 2.17 HABS photos by E. H. Pickering, 1936. Library of Congress.
2.15 Old Sturbridge Village.

2.16 HABS photo by R. M. Lacey, 1937, Library of Congress.
3.1 HABS photo by Edouard Exline, 1935, Library of Congress.
3.2, 4.87 Photos by Jim Broadus.
3.3, 4.91 USDA photo by Knell, National Archives.
3.4, 3.5, 3.6, 3.23 Photos by Bill Morgan.
3.7 Old World Wisconsin, 1980.
3.8 Henry T. Peters Collection, Museum of the City of New York.
3.9 *Harper's Weekly*, 6 January 1877.
3.10 Everson Museum of Art, Syracuse, New York.
3.11 Farm Implement News. 18 August 1898.
3.12 Farm Security Administration photo by M. P. Wolcott, Library of Congress.
3.13, 3.21 From Halstead 1890.
3.14 *American Agriculturalist*, December 1864.
3.22 *Annual Register of Rural Affairs*, 1873.
3.29, 3.30, 3.34, 4.12, 4.21, 4.36 National Archives.
3.31, 3.32 From Ardrey 1894.
3.33 *Farm Implement News*, 22 September 1898.
4.1, 4.5, 4.6, 4.13 Photos by Jim Roe.
4.2, 4.9, 4.43 *Farm Machinery*, 15 December 1903, 20 December 1904, and 13 October 1896, respectively.

4.3, 4.65 *Ohio Farmer*, 31 August 1918.
4.4 From Zintheo 1907.
4.7, 4.44 *Farm Journal*, July 1921, January 1921, respectively.
4.8 Photo by Admire, 1938, National Archives.
4.10, 4.11 John Deere Company Archives.
4.14 Photo by *Des Moines Register and Tribune*, Iowa State Historical Society.
4.15 USDA photo by Forsythe, 1949, National Archives.
4.16, 4.18 Photo by Killian, 1939, National Archives.
4.17 From Crawford 1939.
4.23 *Country Gentlemen*, January 1952.
4.34, 4.35 Drawn by Jim Roe.
4.38, 4.39 Weyerhaeuser Lumber Company.
4.41 From Doane, *Ideas on Farm Buildings*.
4.42 From Halstead 1890.
4.45 *National Lumberman*, July 1930.
4.46, 4.48 Farm Security Administration photo, Library of Congress.
4.51 Photo by Allen G. Noble.
4.98 *USDA Farmer's Bulletin 2076*, 1955.
4.117 Photo by Darlyne H. Kliewer, courtesy of Entertain, Inc. Publishing Company, Lititz, Pennsylvania.

Index

Italics denote illustrations

Agricultural Adjustment Act, 44
Agricultural Adjustment Administration (AAA), 45
Agricultural revolution, 36
Agriculture, commercial, 21
Alley: of double crib, *29-31*,60

Barbacoa, 10
Barns: for corn storage, 14-15, 23, *60*; frontier, 22; Indian, 15; for livestock, 11, 15; Pennsylvania, 13, 15, *61*
Beer, 11-12
Beveled cribbing, *27-28*, 59
Binder, corn, 32, *34*
Birds, problems of, 80-81
Building plans: commercial, 54, *56-57*; custom, 52, 55
Building site, 54
Burbank, Luther, 41

Caches, *7-8*, 9, 12
Carpenters, 12, 50-52
Clay-tile corncribs, 70-72
Colonial farm buildings, lack of illustrations, 17
Colonial farming, 12
Combine corn head, *49*
Commodity Credit Corporation (CCC), 45
Concrete block corncribs, 70, *71-73*
Concrete corncrib, 74, *76*
Construction, 27, 50-54
Cooperatives, farmer, 14
Corn, in Indian diet, 4-5
Corn: migration from Mexico, 4; origin of, 4
Corn, restrictions on use for livestock, 12, 14
Corn, types of, 4

Corn Belt, 22; expansion of, 38
Corncribbing, 26, *27-28*, 59
Corncribs: abandoned, 85-86, 89; airtight, 80; alternative uses of, *83-85*, 86; in art, 14, 17, *18-19*, 23; bin-type, *15-16*, 22, *24*; classic, *16-17*; colonial, 15, *16*, 17; cost of, 56, 58; decorative, *76-77*; experimental, 45, *46-47*; fireproof, *66-73*; geography, 50, 59; at grain elevators, 47; growth of, 46, 50, 63; Indian, *5-6*, 10, 14, 17; largest, *46-48*; origin of, 15-16; outdated by technology, 48-50, 85, 87; pioneer, 15, 22; recycled, *86-87*; styles of, 50-51, *52-57*, 59-61; tearing down, *93*; types, percentages of, 73. *See also* specific types
Corn head, for combines, *49*
Corn houses: colonial, 15, *16*, 17; Indian, 9
Corn picker, 38, *39-40*, 41
Corn picking, by hand: 32, 35; decline of, 49-50
Corn production: colonial, 11-12; Indian, 5; laws, 11
Corn storage, early: in barns, 14, 15; in cache pits, 7-8, 12; in garrets, 9, 14; for security, 14
Cratch, 15, *17*
Cribbing, 26, *27 28*, 59
Crib sheds, 29, *74*
Crib widths, recommended, 78, *80*
Cupolas, design, 51, *52-53*

Depression, economic, 21, 36, 42
Designs, 50-51, *52-57*, 59-61; special, *74-75*
de Soto, Hernando, 5
Doane Building Service, 54, *57*
Dogs: of colonists, 12; of Indians, 5; rat, 83
Double crib: origin of, 29-30, 59-60; and tenancy, 31
Double crib shed, *29-31*, 59-60, *62*
Drying of corn, artificial, 10, 50

Elevator, grain, *41, 42-43*; number of manufacturers, 50
Ever-Normal Granary, 45-*46*; spoilage in, 80
Experiment stations, origin of, 44

Fences, colonial, 11
Fertilizers, 5, 12, 21, 44
Fish, as fertilizer, 5, 12
Foundations of corncribs, problems with, 78-79, 82
Free-enterprise agriculture, early origin, 13

Gable roof, 59, 61, *63*
Gambrel roof, *56*, 61-62, *63*
Garret, for storing corn, 9, 14-15
Gothic roof, *56*, 61-62, *63*
Government farm programs, 44; impact on corncrib construction, 45
Grain drying, artificial, 10, 49-50
Grain elevator. *See* Elevator, grain
Granaries: Mexican, 5, *6-7*; overhead, *47*, *93*; overhead, origin of, 29, 60-61; weight problems of, 78

Harvesters, corn, 32, *35*
Harvesting methods, 23, 49-50
Haysheds, Scandinavian, 13, 16, *17-18*
Hicks, Edward, 17, *18*
Hidley, Joseph, *14*, 17
Historic American Buildings Survey (HABS), 18, *19-20*
Hogs: of colonists, 11-12; corn marketed as, 22; excess production of, 44

Homestead Act, 21, 31
Houses: basement, 14; colonial, 14; as corncribs, 86–87; pioneer, 22
Husker-shredder, corn, 23, *26*
Husking bee, 23, *26*
Husking contests, 33-34
Hybrid corn, 36-37, 41

Iltis, Hugh, 4
Indian corn. *See* Corn
Indian corncribs, 5–6, 10, 14, 17
Indians: corn produced by, 5; storehouses of, *5–6*
Insects, problems of, 80

Jamestown, Virginia, 11
Jones, Donald F., 37

Kalm, Peter, 16
Keystone corncrib, *25*, *27*; origin of, 16–*17*, 22

Land drainage, 21; and expansion of Corn Belt, 38
Laws: colonial, 11–12; federal land disposition, 21; production control, 45
Lawson, John, 10
Livestock, colonial, 11–12
Log corncribs, 5–6, *15*, *20*, 22–23, *26*, 59
Log granaries, Aztec, *5–6*
Lorain, John, 37
Lumber: costs, 27, 56, 58, 63; depletion, 58, 63; hardwood, 56; local supplies, 26–27, 56; mail order, 56, *59*; material list, 54–55; sources of, 27, 56, 58, 63; standards, 58–59; types used, 58; wholesale, 56, 58, 63
Lumberyards, 56, 58

Machinery: dangers of, *39*, *41*, *43*; invented by farmers, 49–*50*; slow development, 32–33; value of, 19th century, 22

Manufactured corncribs, 50, 64; mail order, 56–*58*; metal, *64–69*; wood, *51*, *58*
Maryland, colony of, 12
Masonry corncribs, 70, *71–72*; problems with, 73
Massachusetts, colony of, 11–12
Material list, 54–55
Metal corncribs, *64–70*
Mexico: granaries of, 5, *6–7*; origin for corn, 4
Midwest Farm Plan Service, 54
Mold in corn, problem of, 76, 78, 80
Money, corn as, 12
Mound Builders, of Mississippi valley, 9

New Netherland, colony of, 12

Overhead granary. *See* Granaries, overhead

Picker, corn, 38, *39–40*, 41
Picker-sheller, *49–50*
Pioneer farmers, 21–23
Pioneer Hi-Bred Corn Company, 37
Pit storage, 7, *8*, 9, 12
Plymouth colony, 11–12
Pole corncribs, 54, *57*, *60*
Popcorn crib, 66, *70*
Power take-off (PTO), 39–40
Prairies, problems in settlement, 21–22
Problems in corncribs: in masonry cribs, 73; in metal cribs, 66; and size, 47, 76, *77–79*; and spoilage, 45

Raccoons, problems of, 80
Rafters, 61–62
Rail corncribs, *15–16*, 22, *24*
Ramadas, *5–6*
Rat dogs, 83
Rat poisons, 83
Ratproof corncribs, 66, *67–70*, 71, 81–82

Rats, problems of, 80–83
Roof types, 59–*63*
Rubber tires, 40
Rural carpenters, 50–51

Salvage of lumber, *93–94*
Sawmills, commercial, 27, 56
Scandinavian log haysheds, 16–*17*
Sealed corn, 45–*56*; losses in, 80
Seed corn, 12, *37*; of Indians, 5, 7, 9. *See also* Hybrid corn
Self-feeding corncribs, 54, *58*
Shelled corn, origin of term, 5
Shelling corn, *56*, 83
Shocking, 32–*33*
Shull, George, 37
Siefert, Paul, 17, *19*
Silo, 32
Single crib shed, *62*, 74
Squanto, 12
Square corncrib, 74–75
Steel bins, for shelled corn, 63, *65*, 69
Steel corncribs, *64–70*; and World War I, 66–67
Storage, corn. *See* Corn storage
Storehouses: colonial, 11, 13, *16–17*; Indian, 5–6, 9–10, 12; Swedish, 13
Styles, of corncribs, 50–51; *52–57*, 59–61
Swedish granaries, 13

Tenant farming, 31
Tractor: and corn overproduction, 42; gasoline, 39–*40*; kerosene, *39*
Tree stump corncribs, 22

Underground storage, 7
U.S. Department of Agriculture, 44, *80*
Urban development, and farmsteads, *91–92*

Village-style agriculture, 13-*14*
Virginia colony, storehouse in, 11
V-shaped corncribs, 16-*17*, 22, 30

Wallace, Henry A., 37
Wallace's Granary, 45
Warfarin, rat poison, 83
Weevils, prevention of, 80
Weyerhaeuser Lumber Company, 56, *59*
Whiskey, corn marketed as, 22
Wire mesh cribs, *64, 69*
Women, first American farmers, 5

Yields of corn: by colonists, 12; by Indians, 5

Geographic Index to Illustrations

Finland, 17
Guatemala, 7, 10
Mexico, 6-7
Sweden, 13
United States
  Arizona, 6
  Florida, 9
  Illinois, 8, 24, 46, 53, 56, 64, 77, 92
  Indiana, 15, 60, 70, 81, 90
  Iowa, 37, 39-40, 43, 45-46, 48, 51-55, 61, 63-64, 69, 71-79, 82-83, 85-88, 90-91, 93-95
  Kentucky, 23, 75
  Maryland, 19-20
  Massachusetts, 20
  Minnesota, 17, 24, 29-31, 57, 62, 68, 84-85, 87
  Nebraska, 49, 71
  New Jersey, 20
  New York, 14
  North Carolina, 26
  Ohio, 16, 50, 54, 66-67, 69, 90
  Pennsylvania, 18, 28, 31, 33, 60-62, 77, 81, 86, 89, 91
  Rhode Island, 20
  South Carolina, 61
  Tennessee, 23
  Virginia, 16, 28, 62
  Wisconsin, 18-19, 25, 29, 31-32, 74, 79, 84, 88, 91